Contents

Acknowledgments

I would like to thank all those who replied to my e-mail and telephone messages by sending me material for this book. I have not been able to use all the material sent to me, mainly because of duplication. In particular, I would like to thank the following people for their material and advice on sections of the book: Anneli Silvennoinen, Alle Goldsworthy, Pat Pledger, Paul Pledger, Carol Dunn, Adrian Hodge, George McMurdo, Malcolm Moffat, Ewan Main, Judy Wilkes, Suzette Boyd, Anne-Marie Tarter, Chris Morrison, Laurence O'Donnell, Rob Jones, Mary Day, Duncan Grey, Andy Blizzard, Sally Snowden, Constanza Mekis, Liz Lloyd, Deborah Tate-Smith, Karen Usher, Yvonne Steward, Lynn Barrett, Gerald Brown and Peta Ward.

Thanks also go to Helen Carley, Lin Franklin and the team at LA Publishing for their help and patience.

Finally, love and thanks to Val, Jonathan and Stuart for suffering the travails of yet another book and being so patient and understanding.

James E. Herring

Introduction

The purpose of this book

Writing a book on the Internet for schools may seem to be an exercise in instant obsolescence. Reading some of the literature on the Internet in the form of articles written by Web[1] enthusiasts might give the impression that all new information, ideas and knowledge about the Internet for schools can be found on the Internet itself, thereby making books about the Internet redundant. This is clearly not the case: the Internet does contain a vast array of ideas and information that can be used by schools but those ideas and the relevant information are often not readily available to school librarians and teachers in schools because of the difficulty in searching for information on the Internet. The purpose of this book is provide those working in schools – senior managers, school librarians and teachers – with a guide to exploiting the Internet as an information resource. This book seeks to place the Internet in the educational context of the school curriculum, the technological context of information technology (IT) developments in schools and to examine the use of the Web in particular as a curricular support and as a means to develop information skills in the school. It is not merely a list of interesting websites that might be useful to schools: it seeks to provide a theoretical context for using the Internet and to give examples and case studies of schools that have sought to use the Internet as a tool for learning, teaching and professional development.

The need for this book

Surveys of Internet use in schools such as the Research Machines report that surveyed over 300 schools in the UK in 1997[2] and this author's survey of Internet use in UK and South African school libraries in 1998,[3] show that schools in the developed countries are still at a fairly early stage in fully exploiting the Internet. Most schools have only one or two connections to the Internet and few have access via a network. This situation is likely to change in the next few years, as initiatives such as the UK's 'National Grid for Learning' and similar projects in Australia and North America will provide schools with networked access to the Internet and much lower costs of access. The constant improvement in the capacity of individual personal computers (PCs) will also help to improve the quality of access to the Internet. This book is therefore timely, in that school librarians and teachers, both novices and the more experienced, can benefit from the theoretical context of learning, teaching and information skills; from some aspects of technical knowledge needed to develop use of the Internet; from case studies of how the Web has been used across subject areas as a curricular support; and ideas on developing instructional websites and intranets in schools. This book can therefore be used by school staff to examine their present use of the Internet but also to look forward to further developing their use of the Web and their school network in the future. There is a need for much discussion in schools as to how the Internet is to be used in the curriculum and what professional development is needed by senior management, school librarians and teachers if the Internet is truly to be a means of enriching the school curriculum.

The structure of the book

The first three chapters seek to provide an educational context for exploiting the Internet as an information resource in schools. Although the Internet may be a relatively recent invention and is a new and different resource in schools, its use must be seen in the context of the school curriculum and other IT developments in schools. One of the key themes of this book is how the Internet can be integrated with other learning resources available to pupils,[4] teachers and school librarians. Chapter 2, on the Internet itself, provides an overview of the key elements of using the Internet in schools in relation to areas such as professional development and the structure of the Web. The availability of the Internet provides schools with the opportunity to allow their pupils access to a vast range of potentially useful information resources and so, if pupils are not to be overwhelmed by the sheer amount of information available to them, the teaching of information skills in schools has become even more important than ever. Faced with a range of print resources and CD-ROMs, pupils have often been shown to lack skills in identifying purpose; locating ideas and information; using information in the form of reading for information, note-taking and writing; and self-evaluation of the process. When pupils use the Internet, they will require sophisticated skills in selection and rejection, reading, viewing, listening and understanding. Chapter 3, on information skills, provides guidance on developing information skills for Internet use in particular and using models such as this author's PLUS model.

Chapters 4 to 9 seek to examine how the Internet and the Web in particular can be used within the school curriculum, and each chapter provides a discussion of the ways in which Web resources can be used to enhance the curriculum through the creative use of information-based websites and also instructional websites. These chapters provide examples from schools of aspects such as innovative methods of learning for pupils; developing the role of the school librarian and teacher as facilitator of learning as opposed to deliverer of teaching; integrating Web resources with other information resources in the school; linking different aspects of the curriculum such as history, English and art by using related websites on topics such as World War I; and exploring ways in which school librarians can learn from other schools and discuss ways of jointly developing the use of the Internet in schools. The case studies are illustrative of the work done in some schools but are not presented as ideal models for all schools to follow. One key aspect of the Internet is its internationality, and the case studies and examples show that in many countries across the world schools – often schools in different countries – are sharing ideas from the Web.

Chapters 10 and 11 examine the development of instructional websites in schools and the development of school intranets. The intention here is to present school managers, school librarians and teachers with ideas and examples of how the Internet can both be exploited in schools and serve as the basis for further developments that can add value to the learning and teaching done in schools. Chapter 12 presents some ideas on future developments in this area that schools might consider in their medium- to long-term planning.

Who should read this book?

The book's main focus is on developments in secondary schools (age range 11–18), but those in upper primary schools and in further education (FE) can also benefit from the theory and practice presented. The book is aimed primarily at school librarians and teachers, who are the key players in implementing Internet developments in schools, but it should also be useful to senior management in schools and FE colleges as aspects of school policies – on the curriculum, on information skills and on IT – are discussed in a number of chapters. The themes of integration and cooperation should be of particular interest to school staff of all types, as the case studies show that success in this area is a result of close inter-professional cooperation between a range of staff in schools, including school librarians, teachers and technical staff.

The book will also be of interest to those involved in teaching higher education degree programmes in teacher training and information and library management. Undergraduate and postgraduate students intending to work in schools as teachers, school librarians or technical support staff should also find the book useful.

References

1   The term 'Web' will be used throughout the book to represent the World Wide Web.
2   Research Machines, *The RM report on the Internet in secondary school education*, RM plc, 1998.
3   Survey of school librarians' use of the Internet – to be published.
4   The term 'pupil' will be used in this book to cover those attending school as this term is still used in many UK schools. The author recognizes that many schools now use the term 'student' and that this term is common in other countries. The use of the term 'pupil' is not meant to be seen as derogatory in any way to those attending school.

Chapter 1

IT in schools: an overview

Having read this chapter, you will be able to:

✔ **understand the implications of the National Curriculum and the National Grid for Learning for IT development in UK schools**
✔ **contribute to the development of an IT policy in your school**
✔ **evaluate the use of IT in school administration**
✔ **appreciate the need for IT to be used across the curriculum in schools**
✔ **assess developments and applications of IT in the school library**
✔ **contribute to the development of IT inservice training in your school.**

IT developments in schools

The rapid development of IT in society in general has been reflected in the growth both in the quantity of IT in schools and in the increase in the curricular use of IT in schools. Schools now take the provision of IT as a normal part of their resource portfolio, and within school, there is an ever-increasing demand for more expenditure either to update existing equipment or to purchase new equipment. Thus, in the past few years, there has been an increasing demand on staff in schools not only in learning how to use IT effectively as a teaching and learning tool but also in the administration and management of IT within the school. As networks become the norm in schools, the question of who should be responsible for managing IT becomes problematic when schools cannot afford to employ staff solely to manage IT. The result is that, in many schools, it is left to teachers and the school librarian to form an IT steering group to develop an IT policy and to plan for future use of IT in the school. Financing IT is a major problem for schools, but even when funds are available the extra load placed on staff in terms of managing the installation, development and maintenance of IT is considerable. This chapter addresses some of the key issues by examining the external context of IT in schools, particularly in relation to the UK National Curriculum and the National Grid for Learning; the development of IT policies in schools; the use of IT for administration in schools; the use of IT across the curriculum; current uses of IT in school libraries; and the importance of inservice training (INSET) in schools.

External context of IT in schools

In the UK most schools follow the National Curriculum guidance, though schools in Scotland have separate but very similar curriculum guides. In the National Curriculum at Key Stages 3 and 4 (i.e. relating to secondary schools), pupils' use of IT is defined as 'IT capability', which is seen as 'an ability to use effectively IT tools and information sources to analyse, process and present information, and to model, measure and control external events'.[1] The guidance also indicates that pupils should use IT in problem solving and as a support to learning in different contexts, and that they should be made aware of the effects of IT on society in areas such as employment and telecommunications. Crawford states that there are few detailed references to IT in the National Curriculum but there is a requirement that 'Pupils should be given the opportunities, where appropriate, to develop and apply their IT capability in their study of [the relevant National Curriculum subject]'.[2]

SCAA guidelines

In addition to the statutory guidance provided within the National Curriculum, non-statutory guidance is provided by the UK School Curriculum and Assessment Authority (SCAA) on how IT can be applied in curricular subjects. Crawford states that the National Curriculum does not refer to specific hardware and software but the SCAA identifies types of software, such as word-processing, database and spreadsheet. Crawford argues that in this guidance 'IT is seen as extending what pupils can do, giving them access to a range of information sources and other resources that can be used to support their learning in all subjects'.[3]

The SCAA guidelines identify two themes relating to IT use in schools – 'Communicating and handling information' and 'Controlling, measuring and modelling'. Crawford cites the definition of handling information as pupils use IT 'to collect, sort, classify and store information, and to access, edit, search and analyse it'.[4]

NCET guidance

The National Council for Educational Technology (NCET) also provides non-statutory guidance for schools, giving teachers advice on using IT in the curriculum and how elements of IT use, such as word-processing or desktop publishing, can help pupils complete parts of the Programmes of Study (PoS) in subjects such as English. In one of a series of leaflets relating to subjects in the National Curriculum, the NCET states that, in the history curriculum, IT can help pupils to:

- Ask historical questions
- Investigate change, cause and consequence in history
- Assess and use a wide range of sources
- Organise information and ideas and communicate effectively.[5]

The range of IT activities cited by the NCET leaflet includes the use of databases, CD-ROMs, drawing packages and word-processing software.

Thus it can be seen that teachers and school librarians who use IT themselves and who teach pupils aspects of IT use do so in a context of national curricular guidelines, some of which are statutory. It is clear that one role of the school librarian is to keep all staff in the school up to date with developments relating to the national guidelines by providing information and advice on publications from authorities such as the SCAA and NCET.

National Grid for Learning

The most recent external development relating to the increased use of IT in schools in the UK is the plan to introduce the National Grid for Learning (NGfL). It is particularly interesting to note that the NGfL is viewed by the government as firstly 'A way of finding and using online learning and teaching materials' and only secondly as 'A mosaic of interconnecting networks and education services based on the Internet'.6

This is interesting as it highlights the importance of the *content* of the grid first and the technology of the grid second. The aims of the NGfL are related to raising standards in schools, improving competitiveness in the UK and to literacy and numeracy targets. This is to be achieved through public and private partnerships. The government hopes to 'challenge industry to develop a range of competing managed ICT services aimed initially at schools [and provide] linkage with new initiatives including the People's Lottery funding for ICT teacher and librarian training'.7 The aim of the government is to have all schools connected to the grid by 2002; specific targets are stated, including the intention to provide 75% of teachers and 50% of all pupils with their own e-mail address and file space by that year. The NGfL guidelines state that, in order to qualify for support, schools should 'formulate plans for their use of ICT across the curriculum . . . for staff development and administration'.8

The NGfL proposal document includes the aim of establishing a virtual teacher centre that can be accessed via the Internet.9 This centre will focus on the needs of school management teams, teachers and 'staff responsible for library and resource centre management'. It will provide schools with access to online versions of the school curriculum, websites that guide teachers on the use of ICT (Information and Communication Technology)s in the curriculum, a virtual language teaching centre and links to government websites. Thus the virtual teacher centre is potentially a very valuable resource for schools and, if properly managed and funded, could lead to a much greater sharing of ideas and resources by school librarians and teachers in the UK and elsewhere.

However, Kenny strikes a note of caution, arguing that there are fears that the NGfL will 'encapsulate everything that most teachers dislike: a top-down approach, predetermined paths, uniformity, rigidity'.10 He also states that the government will have to ensure that the consortia set up to provide the Grid and its content will not stifle choice and innovation in schools, and he argues that the virtual teacher centre 'has to be more than just a list of Web links; there has to be content to intrigue, to make life easier, to spread expertise and to stimulate',[11] and that the Grid must be accompanied by adequate inservice training for teachers and school librarians.

Developing IT policies in schools

The NCET states that 'A whole school IT policy is a statement of the beliefs, values and goals of a school staff working cooperatively in the context of using IT in the operation of the school'.[12]

Heinrich argues that an IT policy for a school must be seen as part of the school's overall planning, and states that 'The school development plan is the basic instrument for the ongoing development of a school and all other planning must recognise and support the strategies set out in that document'.[13] Thus within the school development plan, according to Heinrich, IT should be addressed 'not only within the curriculum strand but also under personnel, resources and buildings . . . IT should be at the heart of the school development plan'.[14] Tagg concurs with this view, stating that 'It is not appropriate to have a school IT policy which is isolated from the development plan as a whole'.[15]

Hackett and Kennedy state that

> the IT policy is a philosophical statement which focuses on what the school feels that IT adds to the pupils' learning in the school environment. It states the benefits of an IT experience for pupils and indicates how pupils will receive their entitlement to IT and thus develop their IT ability. It should reflect current good practice, new technology and future needs.[16]

Thus, Hackett and Kennedy argue, the IT policy should be a vision which is shared by all staff in the school; it should indicate the school's strategic plans for IT development and the policy should 'reflect the ethos, aims, objectives of the school as a whole [and] .. should focus on learning and how IT can enhance this by integrating the policy work into initiatives'.[17]

Role of the headteacher

Donnelly argues that the headteacher has a crucial role to play in ensuring that the school has an IT policy and that the policy is put into practice across the school. He cites the NCET's statement that 'the attitude of the headteacher is the most important factor in influencing attitudes towards computers and IT in the school. If computers are ignored or merely accepted by the headteacher, they will be marginalised within the school'.[18]

Donnelly cites five ways in which the headteacher can promote IT within the school: the headteacher should:

✔ be seen to be using IT in teaching and administration
✔ encourage the development of IT in the school via an 'IT leader' who might be the deputy head
✔ allocate sufficient funding to IT in the school, perhaps by using ring-fencing
✔ encourage the development of inservice training for IT for *all* school staff
✔ ensure that IT is used across the curriculum and that there is a balance of IT resources across the school.[19]

Before an IT policy in a school can be developed, it is important that the school carries out an audit of IT within the school as a whole. Tagg argues that an IT audit is

> not just a question of knowing how many computers the school has and how old they are (although this is part of it). School management also needs to know the level of commitment for these computers for this year and for future years . . . More important still, schools need to know where their expertise lies and where it needs to be built up.[20]

IT audit

Smith provides guidelines for conducting an IT audit and states that schools should conduct an audit of software within the school; this should be a survey that is qualitative as well as quantitative in nature. Thus each department should be asked to rate the software in terms of its being essential for all pupils, widely used but not essential, seldom used by pupils or used by teachers only. Future needs should also be investigated. Smith argues that an audit of curricular use of IT should identify the actual use of IT in the classroom, the school library and elsewhere in the school and not merely what is in the school IT policy. This audit also needs to be a check on whether the school meets the National Curriculum requirements for IT. Smith states that a review of hardware should not merely measure the number of computers and peripherals in the school but should concentrate on 'the extent to which the school's equipment provision is supporting its curriculum aims [and] how well the school's equipment provision is supporting its curricular aspirations'.[21]

It is further argued that a school can be very well equipped with IT but may not make very good curricular use of its IT resources. Smith identifies the steps for effectively carrying out an IT audit as:

- An analysis of software usage
- IT strand profiles
- Subject penetration profiles
- Notes and statistics of the hardware base
- Notes and statistics on standards and quality
- Issues sheet.[22]

The IT audit report should include, Smith recommends, an analysis of what standards are being achieved, how IT contributes to the quality of learning in the school, the extent to which the National Curriculum IT requirements are being met and whether hardware, software and staffing resources are adequate to support the curriculum.[23]

IT policy content

In relation to the content of an IT policy in a school, Crawford states that the policy should cover areas such as how IT is managed in the school, how the IT curriculum is organized, how IT is used in the monitoring and assessment of pupils' work, how hardware and software are provided and managed in the school, how equal opportunity of access and use is ensured, what staff are needed to manage IT, what INSET is provided and how IT developments are to be funded. Crawford argues that the IT policy needs to be reviewed on a yearly basis because of changes in technology and costs.[24]

Heinrich argues that an IT policy should contain the following:

- aims and objectives
- a set of the minimum IT requirements set out in the National Curriculum which the school must meet
- a clear indication of the software required for these activities, its suitability for pupils of particular abilities and machine configurations

- procedures for gaining access to hardware in order for these activities to take place
- the hardware development programme
- the software development programme
- the inservice training programme
- a statement on progression and coherence (which may be the same as that in the [overall] school policy)
- information on how IT capability will be assessed
- a projection (in outline) of probable developments in subsequent years of the policy
- a date for review of the policy.[25]

Hackett and Kennedy also produce guidelines for the production of an IT policy document and recommend that a draft document is written by the IT coordinator. This should then be scrutinized by an IT committee, made up of representatives of senior management and departments, that should examine the policy in relation to National Curriculum requirements, current IT resources, and IT priorities in the school. This will result in a working document that can be presented to governors and all staff for comment. The agreed policy should then be issued to all staff, and Hackett and Kennedy recommend a yearly review of the policy. They also argue that the school should draw up an IT development plan that outlines the key areas of development over the next three years. This should be followed by an IT action plan that details how the IT policy will be implemented in terms of resources, timescales, staffing and responsibilities. The final plan recommended by Hackett and Kennedy is an IT business plan, which should include financial projections and the implications of implementing the IT policy.[26]

Donnelly argues that an IT policy should answer a series of questions, including:

- Who is responsible for policy development?
- What are the aims of IT use in the school?
- What is the present curricular provision of IT in the school?
- Where are the computers sited?
- What are the specific objectives for the development of IT in the school and what is the timescale to achieve them?
- What is the role of the IT coordinator?

• What resources will be made available to develop the objectives of an IT policy?[27]

The role of the headteacher has been shown to be vital in terms of leadership in relation to the formulation of a school IT policy; the next key role in the school's IT development is that of the IT coordinator. The person designated as the school's IT coordinator may well be a member of the computer studies department, but in some schools this role is taken by a subject teacher in another department. In a minority of schools the school librarian acts as IT coordinator because of the up-to-date IT skills that she possesses. Tagg argues that this post should be referred to as IT manager and not coordinator because of the management skills needed. The holder of the post is envisaged as 'leading and instigating as well as holding IT education together – an appointment [should be made] at a fairly senior level'. Tagg states that the person appointed needs to be a good communicator in the school and does not need to be a technocrat, but does need a certain level of technical expertise.[28]

Donnelly distinguishes between the IT leader in the school, who is likely to be a member of the senior management team, and the IT coordinator, who will be responsible for implementing the IT policy but who will report to the IT leader. Donnelly argues that the IT coordinator needs to have very good interpersonal skills in dealing with staff, advanced technical skills and organizational skills to coordinate IT across the curriculum.[29]

Role of the school librarian

The development of an IT policy is a prerequisite of managing a modern secondary school, and, as indicated above, it should be seen as one of the most important policies within the school's overall plan. The role of the school librarian in relation to the school IT policy can take a number of forms. A passive role would be to provide information required for the development of IT within the library, e.g. CD-ROM provision, or to find information for senior management, e.g. costs of hardware or software. However, many school librarians take a much more proactive role and view the opportunity to contribute to IT policy development as a means of highlighting the importance of the library in the school and as a means of demonstrating their own knowledge and skills in IT. This enables them to be seen as IT experts in the school and therefore capable of contributing to overall school IT policy and not merely to policy relating to IT in the library. School librarians can therefore play an important information role, e.g. by searching the literature for IT policy guidelines or the Internet for examples of school IT policies. They can also contribute to discussion on policy relating to the development of school networks and intranets in the context of learning and teaching in the school.

IT and school administration

Crawford identifies a range of applications of IT in school administration and management. These include lists of pupils, which can be stored and used to produce class lists, as well as other reports. Records of attendance can identify 'patterns of absence for individual pupils, a group of pupils, a particular class or year group . . . Letters to parents can be generated, informing them of their child's absences and this information can be summarised for the relevant members of staff and education welfare officers'.[30] Where schools use methods such as swipe cards to record attendance, Crawford notes, there is often a drop in absenteeism. Pupils' records of achievements and progress can be recorded and can be integrated into pupil reports using OMR (optical mark recognition) and a bank of statements. Pupils' entries for external examinations can be recorded and the results analysed in relation to individuals or class groups. Databases with information relating to the National Curriculum and courses in higher or further education can be used to provide better access to information for teachers and pupils. Crawford also refers to personnel records, which can include 'financial forecasting of the school's staff costs, audits of teachers' skills and knowledge, the planning of staff development and whole school development planning'.[31]

The school timetable can also be automated using software to coordinate teachers, pupils and classrooms as well as ad hoc activities such as parents' evenings and school examinations. Finally, Crawford refers to the use of IT in financial planning and administration in the school and states that 'A well established system will provide a sound basis for forecasting, planning and analysis, including 'what if' modelling.[32]

Information systems

Crawford's analysis of IT in school administration is supported by Pitts who argues that 'Well constructed information is the key to any successful management system'.[33] The introduction of local financial management (LFM) led local education authorities (LEAs) to examine schools' information needs, according to Pitts, in relation to:

- the current data held
- the flow of information
- the data analysis that would be needed
- the data that would need to be held for the future
- the type of information outputs that would be required.[34]

It is argued that each school needs a relational database that integrates access to a range of factors, including pupils, the curriculum, staff, finance and resources. The system installed needs to allow retrieval from one or more of the factors and produce a variety of reports. Pitts states that 'Pupil data consists of a mass of personal information whose breadth and quality will determine the value of the system and its applications.'[35]

Finally, Pitts makes the crucial point that the sophistication of the technology will not necessarily equal the sophistication in the use of information put into or taken out of the system. She argues that 'IT tools provide us with a wealth of support for information handling and decision making. What is important is that we use information as a resource to manage effectively'.[36]

The use of IT in school administration has grown from the use of word-processing in the school office to the use of financial modelling packages by senior management in planning school developments. While there are many positive elements in the use of IT in school administration, Crawford points out some problems that can arise: these include the costs of management information systems (MIS) and the need for training, the compatibility of software from different suppliers, the lack of sufficient hardware to provide access across the school, and unauthorized access to confidential files. Crawford notes the importance of the UK Data Protection Act for schools as the act means that schools have to register the purposes for which they keep information on pupils and staff.[37]

The development of school intranets (see Chapter 11) will mean that administrative information, ranging from timetables to confidential staff and pupil files, will be available across the school from any point in the school network. School managers will therefore have to ensure that adequate security is included in the school's intranet to prevent unauthorized access. The use of IT in school administration and management allows senior management and school staff to manage a range of information more effectively and to produce professional reports (e.g. for parents or pupils) that include added value information.

IT across the curriculum

Curriculum models

The debate surrounding the teaching of IT in secondary schools has continued since the late 1980s. It is interesting to note that this author noted virtually the same discussions on IT across the curriculum as those taking place currently in his book *Information technology in schools*[38] published in 1992. Hackett and Kennedy identify three models of delivering IT teaching in schools. The first is the 'discrete information technology' model: 'This is where time is allocated on the timetable for a subject called Information Technology. These lessons usually take place in a specialist IT room and are generally taught by an IT specialist.'[39]

The key advantages of this model are that it ensures that pupils fulfil the IT requirements of the National Curriculum (or equivalent); assessment of pupils' achievements in relation to IT entitlement and capability is facilitated; it is easier to timetable as the teaching is done by one group of staff; and activities from other subjects such as art, mathematics or history can be integrated. However, Hackett and Kennedy state that this model has disadvantages: for example, 'Activities using IT may be delivered without a context and pupils will be less able to transfer their skills.'[40]

In addition, IT resources may not be spread across school departments: this may limit both the potential of IT as a cross-curricular resource and the acquisition of IT skills by other staff. Crawford notes similar problems with this model, and states that 'It has been suggested that the subject IT approach is unlikely to provide sufficiently rich contexts in which pupils can consolidate their IT skills'.[41]

The second Hackett and Kennedy model is 'A short course of IT/Core skills', in which pupils are given a short but intensive course in IT skills that are subsequently reinforced in other subject areas by means of agreement with the IT coordinator and subject teachers. The advantages of this model include the fact that 'Mapping of pupils' IT experiences in both IT lessons and subjects of the curriculum can be used to provide good evidence of continuity and progression',[42] and also that subject teachers will develop IT skills through this model. The clear obstacle to the success of this model becomes apparent if subject teachers do not acquire the requisite skills through INSET.

The third model is 'Cross-curricular IT', which implies that IT skills are taught solely through the subject areas and the requirements of the National Curriculum (or equivalent) are met by spreading them across subjects; for example, handling information may be taught in history. Hackett and Kennedy argue that it is vital that IT use in all subjects is monitored to ensure that all pupils receive their entitlement, and that IT is seen as integral to the subject's scheme of work. The key advantages of this model are that pupils can develop IT skills in a range of subject areas and that more teachers will gain IT expertise via this model.[43] Crawford notes that possible disadvantages may arise if IT teaching is perceived to add to the existing workload or if there is a lack of expertise amongst subject teachers. Crawford suggests that most schools operate a hybrid approach, and he suggests that in an ideal hybrid model 'pupils are taught and assessed by an IT specialist in IT subject classes and use IT across the curriculum where possible'.[44] Corbett provides an example of a hybrid model from Brakendale School, and argues that before pupils can use IT in subject areas they must be taught by specialist IT staff. These specialists can then liaise with subject teachers to ensure that the skills are taught at a subject level also and that at the end of Key Stage 3 (year 3 of secondary school) pupils are able to identify how IT can be an aid to their work in their own subject areas.[45]

Each school will have to develop its own version of one of the models above, and the model chosen may depend on the availability of expertise across the school. It is important that, within the teaching of IT in the curriculum, use is made of the school library as an example of where a range of IT skills (but particularly information handling skills) can be learned and applied. Also, in some schools, the school librarian is an integral part of the teaching team responsible for IT in different areas of the curriculum. Where school librarians make their own expertise known within the school, good use can be made of this by subject teachers and pupils, but in many cases it may be up to the school librarian to make a case for inclusion in this teaching team.

IT in school libraries

Jones argues that the role of the school librarian is to provide pupils and teachers with 'the right information at the right time', and that this includes the provision of fiction, reference works and leisure reading as well as information in an electronic form. Jones states that the development and use of IT must be a key part of the library's development plan and that the use of IT in the school library must fit in with the school's overall IT policy. It is the combination of both print and electronic resources that provides the key to the provision of an effective information service to the school, and the modern school librarian needs a combination of technical and information resource knowledge and skills to exploit all the resources available.[46]

CD-ROMs

For many school libraries, the introduction of CD-ROMs was the first time that IT was used to provide an information resource to pupils and teachers; CD-ROMs today are still the key source of electronic information in most school libraries. With better and cheaper access to the Internet this is likely to change in the next few years, but CD-ROMs are unlikely to disappear in the near future. They are now regarded as an integral part of the modern school library's information resources and represent a valuable addition to the school library. CD-ROMs first appeared in schools in the form of encyclopedias such as Encarta and Grolier, which have become more sophisticated with each new edition. CD-ROM encyclopedias have the advantages of being easy to search and of being able to provide text, graphics, photographs and video clips and are therefore more easy to use than their printed counterparts. Whether they represent a key *curricular* resource will depend on the effective use of information by pupils.

CD-ROM newspapers are likely to be seen as a much more curriculum-related information source in the school library. In the UK, national broadsheets such as the Guardian, regional newspapers such as the Scotsman, tabloid newspapers such as the Daily Record and some local newspapers can now be purchased in CD-ROM format. For subjects that demand that pupils use reasonably up-to-date material, such as business, modern and media studies, CD-ROM newspapers have an immediate attraction. However, newspapers on CD-ROM can also be useful in science subjects via reports on scientific developments, history via articles on historical events, geography via reports on urban or rural development and English in the form of book reviews or comparative reports of the same event in different newspapers. Searching newspaper CD-ROMs will provide relevant and up to date material if the pupil's search strategy is well constructed.

Subject-based CD-ROMs

The main advance in CD-ROMs recently is the increase in the number of subject-based CD-ROMs being produced. In the UK many of these are designed to fit in with the key stages of the National Curriculum and therefore have direct relevance to the school curriculum. Subject-based CD-ROMs are available in all subjects and represent a real advance in the range and quality of curriculum-related information resources in the school. One of the roles of the school librarian is to scan the literature for reviews of CD-ROMs, and make teachers aware of such reviews as well as the less-biased features in publishers' catalogues. Subject-based CD-ROMs, such as those covering Shakespeare's plays, present pupils with information and ideas in different forms. Thus pupils can read the text of a play, listen to the actors' voices, watch clips from scenes in the play, listen to interviews about the play and use the hyperlinks in the text to seek explanations for individual words or passages of text.

Relevance to the curriculum

The availability of CD-ROMs at relatively cheap prices means that schools can provide access to a vastly increased *amount* of information in the school library; the range of sources that pupils can use for research on curricular topics is also widened. However, amount does not take into account quality or relevance to the curriculum. The latter should be the first criterion when deciding whether to purchase a

CD-ROM. Relevance to the curriculum can mean that a CD-ROM is useful for a particular level in the school or that it relates well to existing resources – books, journals, newspapers, etc. – that pupils already use. School librarians and teachers need to examine the needs of their own school and its curriculum: a CD-ROM on volcanoes may be ideal for one school at secondary level 3 but not for another.

Criteria for selection

Relevance to the curriculum will be considered along with the level of language used to determine the usefulness of a CD-ROM. For some pupils, an encyclopedia article on volcanoes may be too difficult either at a conceptual level or because of the terminology used, whereas a CD-ROM specifically designed for secondary level 3 geography should contain a level of vocabulary suitable for those pupils. CD-ROMs are likely to be used to *support* the curriculum and to be used after pupils have been introduced to concepts and terminology in the classroom. Thus it is very important that pupils do not meet too many new concepts or terms that are unfamiliar to them when they use the CD-ROM.

CD-ROMs should also be user-friendly in terms of accessing different parts of the CD-ROM or searching for particular keywords, phrases, names or illustrations. CD-ROMs should allow pupils – and indeed encourage them – to use Boolean logic in terms of 'AND', 'OR' and 'NOT' when searching. In some CD-ROMs particular aspects will be more important. For example, in art CD-ROMs, such as the recently published (1998) Thames and Hudson products *The age of Breugel* and *The age of Rembrandt*, the ability of pupils to zoom in on paintings is a key feature of the product; this provides added value in that pupils would not be able to study features of the painting in such detail in the art gallery. In other CD-ROMs, such as the recently published *London Docklands* (1998), teachers can insert questions or tasks for pupils in windows next to particular sections of the CD-ROM.

In today's schools, pupils are accustomed, both in the school and at home, to using multimedia products of high quality that contain sophisticated features in terms of graphics, photographs, video-clips and sound. The pupils thus have high expectations in terms of quality – much higher than they would have if using printed materials. Thus the CD-ROMs selected need to have these same sophisticated features if they are to be attractive to pupils. This is a difficult problem for school librarians and teachers in that to them it is the *content* of the CD-ROMs that is most important and not the 'gloss factor' associated with entertainment CD-ROMs. Pupils can be made aware of this and persuaded not to treat CD-ROMs in the library in the same way as the entertainment CD-ROMs they may have in their homes.

A final aspect of CD-ROMs to be considered relates to culture. The first encyclopedias to appear on CD-ROM were particularly criticized by those outside the USA for the dominance of American culture in the content. This not only related to spelling and the use of dialect words but also to the way other countries and cultures were represented. Thus, when choosing CD-ROMs, school librarians and teachers will need to be aware of such possible cultural, racial, political and religious bias. A useful website relating to CD-ROM criteria is at **http://www.icbl.hw.ac.uk/icbl/icbl-background.html**.

Online information sources

A minority of school libraries in developed countries have recently had access to some commercially available online information resources; in the UK, the Reuters Media and Advertising Briefing service has been available at low cost to schools. One of the most useful features of the Reuters package is the global five-year archive of news stories from 2000 newspapers, newswires, and business and general interest journals from around the world. There is a wide variety of search strategies that can be used when pupils or teachers are using the News Archive. Firstly, topics can be searched within the displayed lists on the screen (Figure 1.1). Thus pupils can select the combination of countries, industries, companies, topics and sources that suits their particular information need. For example, a pupil could search for news stories on aspects of cable and satellite television in the UK and Australia for a project relating to Rupert Murdoch. By highlighting the required countries and topic and choosing a source (in this case Reuters as opposed to any specific newspaper or journal), the pupil will be able to search over a specified period for stories relating to his or her topic. When the search is completed, the pupil can scan through the retrieved articles and select the most appropriate i.e. those that match the needs of the pupil's project.

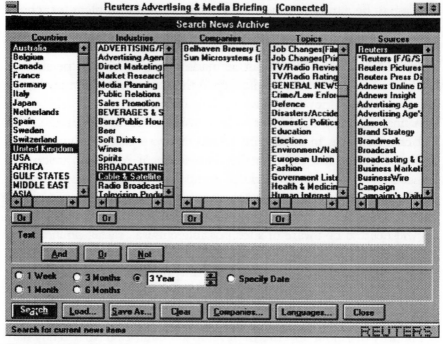

Fig. 1.1   *Searching for topics using the Reuters online service*

One key advantage of the Reuters service in schools is that teachers can download searches and use the same articles with pupils in future lessons. Thus the Reuters archive can help to establish a school archive of downloaded articles that can be used for teaching purposes, taking account of any copyright restrictions that may apply on the reproduction of articles.[47]

Library management systems

The use of automated library management systems in school libraries has increased greatly in recent years because of the development of new systems suitable for small libraries and the decrease in the cost of such systems. Jones notes that the Heritage system used at Carisbrooke High School provides pupils with access to information on books, journals, software, CD-ROMs, maps and portable hardware, and provides the librarian with time-saving control over stock as well as the ability to provide a range of management statistics relating to use of the library.[48] The Alice system has recently been developed to allow school librarians across the world to provide access to websites via the school library catalogue. Thus a pupil searching the catalogue will retrieve a range of resources including books and CD-ROMs, but can also retrieve web-site URLs (uniform resource locators), which can be accessed directly by clicking on the URL. The Alice system then links with the school's Internet software so that the pupil can search the actual website. Figure 1.2 shows an example of an Alice search and Figure 1.3 shows the results of choosing the Web resource, 'The ABCs of acid rain'.

The use of the Internet in the school library is a natural progression from the use of CD-ROMs, online services and automated library sys-tems. School librarians around the world are exploiting these electronic information resources to provide an *integrated* information service to their users. Subsequent chapters in this book will explore the enor-mous potential of using the Internet in the school as a whole as well as in the school library, though a key issue for school librarians and teach-ers relates to the importance of encouraging pupils to view all infor-mation resources as having curricular relevance and teaching pupils how to discriminate between the different resources they might need, depending on their immediate task.

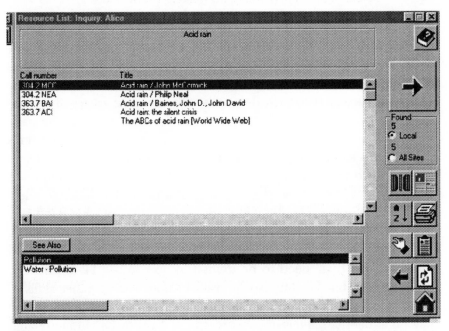

Fig. 1.2   *Using Alice library management system to find information on acid rain*

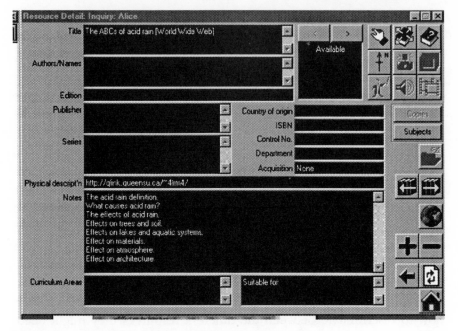

Fig. 1.3   *A Web resource identified by the Alice system*

Inservice training (INSET) for IT in schools

As has been seen above, one of the key problems identified in teaching IT in schools and in ensuring an even spread of IT expertise across the school relates to the lack of INSET for subject teachers in many schools. For teachers to provide pupils with adequate advice and training in the use of IT in subject areas, it will be vital that teachers have the confidence in their own expertise to be able to transfer such skills to pupils in a subject context. Thus if a history teacher is going to teach pupils how to create a small database of local history information, the teacher will require knowledge not only of a particular database package available in the school but also some knowledge of what databases can be used for, how they are designed and what their limitations are.

Donnelly identifies two aspects of IT training within schools, and states that 'Staff will need to be trained in how to use IT to enhance pupil learning but IT can also be used to train staff in other skills'.[49] He argues that schools can use a mixture of external courses (which may be expensive), internal courses (which must to be closely related to the needs of *that* school) and cascade training, in which expert teachers train other staff often in conjunction with the use of the tutorials that are a feature of most software packages.

Motivation

Crawford emphasizes the importance of motivating teachers to acquire IT skills, and that teachers will give more priority to IT if the school's senior management identify IT as a priority area and if the IT policy values the use of IT across the curriculum. Crawford also suggests that schools devote complete INSET days to IT skills acquisition and discussion about teaching IT in subject areas. Training, it is argued, can help teachers, school librarians and other staff develop:

- an understanding of the dynamic of whole school planning for IT
- an understanding of the cross curricular nature of IT
- an appreciation of the use of IT in a range of subjects
- an awareness of the range of CAL software available
- an ability to evaluate software and CD-ROMs etc for use in the classroom.[50]

School librarians and INSET

For school librarians, INSET can mean the opportunity to learn new skills in using IT for information retrieval, the identification of curricular resources or for administration in the school library. INSET can also be an opportunity to play the role of trainer by running INSET sessions on the use of CD-ROMS or the Internet in the classroom and in the school library. For their own personal IT development, many school librarians now have to rely on self-help or in-school INSET with teachers because the support previously provided by school library services is no longer available. The use of professional journals such as the UK's *School libraries in view* can provide guidelines and examples for school librarians to follow to ensure that they are not left behind by IT developments in their school or in their profession as a whole.

Conclusion

There is and will continue to be pressure on schools to adapt to the changes in technology that appear constantly. Schools have to both adopt new technologies for educational purposes and resist the pressure to install the latest hardware or software merely because it is available. IT is a tool that schools can use to enhance learning and teaching: school management, teachers and school librarians will ensure that IT *is* used for this purpose by examining firstly the school's educational needs, policies and priorities and, secondly the extent to which IT can contribute to the pupils' educational development. Pupils do need to acquire IT skills but some of these skills are fairly mechanical. For example, the ability to open a spreadsheet package, enter data and produce tables or pie charts is a valuable skill for a pupil to have, but the key learning requirements associated with spreadsheets are related to that pupil's use of data analysed within a spreadsheet e.g. to solve a problem. Thus school IT policies will highlight a range of learning skills that pupils can acquire or develop using IT as well as the basic IT skills in using software packages. All school staff will need to acquire IT skills but, as with the pupils, staff will have to examine how such skills can enhance their own learning and teaching. INSET will be required to provide teachers and school librarians with new skills, but it also needs to provide time for such staff to reflect on the use of IT in their own departments and to determine their own future needs. For school librarians, future needs will include their knowledge of the Internet, of school networks and of the implications of networked learning for the school and the school library.

References

1 Crawford, R., *Managing information technology in secondary schools*, London, Routledge, 1997.
2 ibid.
3 ibid.
4 School Curriculum and Assessment Authority, *An introduction to the revised national curriculum*, SCAA, 1995, in Crawford, R., op. cit.
5 Department for Education and Employment, *Connecting the learning society: national grid for learning*, London, DfEE, 1997.
6 ibid.
7 ibid.
8 ibid.
9 ibid.
10 Kenny, J., 'A fair share of the Web', *Times educational supplement online education*, 9 January 1998.

11 ibid.
12 National Council for Educational Technology, Information sheet on IT policy, Coventry, NCET, 1996.
13 Heinrich, P., 'The school development plan for IT', in Tagg, B. (ed.), *Developing a whole school IT policy*, London, Pitman, 1995.
14 ibid.
15 Tagg, B., op. cit.
16 Hackett, S. and Kennedy, B. *Managing school IT*, Cambridge, Pearson Publishing, 1996.
17 ibid.
18 Donnelly, J., *IT and schools*, London, Croner, 1996.
19 ibid.
20 Tagg, B., op. cit.
21 Smith, M., 'The IT audit', in Tagg, B., op. cit.
22 ibid.
23 ibid.
24 Crawford, R., op. cit.
25 Heinrich, P., op. cit.
26 Hackett, S. and Kennedy, B., op. cit.
27 Donnelly, J., op. cit.
28 Tagg, B., op. cit.
29 Donnelly, J., op. cit.
30 Crawford, R., op. cit.
31 ibid.
32 ibid.
33 Pitts, H., 'The school office', in Tagg, B., op. cit.
34 ibid.
35 ibid.
36 ibid.
37 Crawford, R., op. cit.
38 Herring, J. E. (ed.), *Information technology in schools*, London, Library Association Publishing, 1992.
39 Hackett, S. and Kennedy, B., op. cit.
40 ibid.
41 Crawford, R., op. cit.
42 Hackett, S. and Kennedy, B., op. cit.
43 ibid.
44 Crawford, R., op. cit.

45 Corbett, A., 'How can you integrate IT across the curriculum?', *Computers don't bite*, January 1998.

46 Jones, R., 'The management of resources – IT in the library', *School libraries in view*, (6), Autumn 1996, 3–5.

47 Herring, J. E.,'Press for action', *Educational computing and technology*, May 1998, 49–51.

48 Jones, R., op. cit.

49 Donnelly, J., op. cit.

50 Crawford, R., op. cit.

Chapter 2
The Internet

Having read this chapter, you will be able to:

✔ evaluate the Internet as a professional resource for school staff

✔ use search engines to find relevant information on the Web

✔ use a range of criteria to evaluate curriculum related websites

✔ apply the principles of copyright when using the Web

✔ learn from school-related Internet projects.

The ubiquitous Internet

The Internet is now the topic of much debate within the developed world. Even those who have never used the Internet will be aware of its existence because of coverage in newspapers either in the form of supplements, such as the *Online Guardian* or the *Daily Telegraph's Connected*, or in mainstream news stories. It is also visible on TV when there are news stories of computer fraud or pornography on the Internet; many TV adverts now include website information as do some TV programmes. On the radio, news, discussion or music programmes now regularly give out the programme's e-mail address to attract listener participation in debates or requests for music to be played. An increasing number of people have Internet connections in their homes and are regular users of e-mail or the Web either for business purposes, recreation or as a substitute for letters and telephone calls in communication with relatives or friends. Businesses now have Internet use built into their companies' infrastructure; *not* having an e-mail address or website can often be seen as a commercial disadvantage, similar to the lack of a fax number. The Internet has created many new companies whose business is to create websites for clients or to sell information or goods via a website. This 'electronic commerce' is becoming a major part of Western economies as businesses see new opportunities to reach bigger markets by using the Web. While there is much exaggerated praise for the Internet, such as 'The Internet is the greatest and most significant achievement in the history of mankind',[1] it is also much criticized with some expressing fears that a new generation of 'screenagers' is being created. These are adolescents who spend much of their leisure time on the Web for recreational purposes but who conduct this activity on their own despite being in touch with others electronically.

Given the increasing availability of the Internet in society in general, it is logical that schools should also try to harness the benefits (and avoid the pitfalls) of such a potentially revolutionary technology. As with all new technologies (e.g. tape-slides in the 1970s, video in the 1980s) schools will aim to ensure that the Internet is seen and used as an *educational* tool that supports the school curriculum, can benefit senior management and school staff, including teachers and school librarians, and can enhance the learning process for pupils. It is in this context that the Internet has to be judged in schools despite its recreational and business use in society in general. This chapter will briefly cover the origins and structure of the Internet and will then examine e-mail and listservs as professional resources for school librarians and teachers; how the Web works; search engines and their use in schools; the evaluation of websites; downloading websites; copyright and the Web; the need for acceptable use policies in schools; and a review of school related Internet projects in the UK.

The Internet defined

Winship and McNab state: 'Simply put, the Internet is an international network of computer networks – it links millions of computers around the world, and can be used for many different and ever growing purposes'.[2] Another definition is provided in *Computers don't bite*, which says that 'In a nutshell, [the Internet] is a world-wide network of computers, all linked together via telephone lines. However, the Internet is not just about computers, it is really about people talking and sharing information'.[3] The Internet began in the 1970s and had military origins. The US Department of Defense needed to link its military research network called ARPAnet to some of its other networks. The

use of these linked networks spread to universities and research insti-
tutes in the USA, and this was followed by links to Europe and the rest
of the world. The Internet has grown at a phenomenal rate and it has
been estimated that 300 new organizations and users join the Internet
every *hour*.

E-mail and listservs as professional resources

The use of e-mail by teachers, school librarians and pupils is increasing rapidly. As was noted above, in the UK the government hopes to
provide all school staff and pupils with individual e-mail addresses by
2002. E-mail or electronic mail, is a means of communicating with
another person or group of people via a computer. It is the electronic
equivalent of the postal service in that each user has an individual
address and will send messages to another user or group of users at
their individual addresses. For example, this author's e-mail address is
j.herring@mail.qmced.ac.uk. This is made up of the user's name
and his or her 'address'. In this case, the author's address is given following the @, and can be translated as the mail server at Queen
Margaret College, Edinburgh (qmced), which is a university (ac) in the
UK (uk). This address can be used by anyone in the world who wishes
to communicate with the author via e-mail. Figure 2.1 shows an example of an e-mail message sent to the author by a contact in Australia.

Using e-mail

The e-mail box contains the address of the person sending the message
('From'), the address of the recipient ('To'), an indication of the content of the message ('Subject') and the exact date and time when the
message was sent. Above the message box, there are a number of icons
that can be used to reply to the message, forward it to another user,
move it to a folder (i.e. a file of e-mail messages that the user wishes to
keep), a facility to send an attachment (e.g. a word-processed document) to another user, a delete button that can be used to delete the
message if it is not needed once it has been read, a print button if the
user wishes to print out a message and buttons that can take the user
to the next or previous message. When a user logs in to the e-mail system, normally by means of a password, s/he is presented with a list of
messages that have been received but have not been read. Figure 2.2

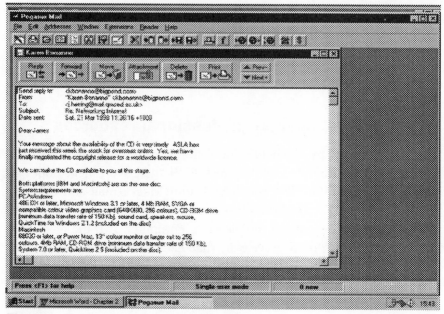

Fig. 2.1   *E-mail message sent to the author*

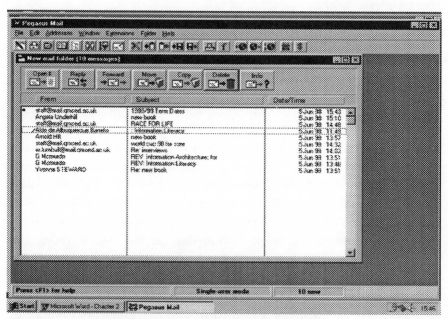

Fig. 2.2   *List of e-mail messages received by the author*

shows an example of a list of e-mail messages waiting to be read by the author.

Listservs

LM_NET

E-mail can be a professional resource for school librarians and teachers in that they can exchange information with colleagues inside the school or contact fellow professionals outside the school, e.g. with questions about teaching methods or with information relating to resources such as books or CD-ROMs. The sharing of professional information is greatly enhanced when school librarians and teachers take part in electronic discussion groups, called listservs. For school librarians in the United States (and elsewhere) the main listserv is LM_NET, which provides a forum for the exchange of information relating to topics of interest to school librarians and educators in general. Individual users join the listserv by sending a message to the listserv's host computer. Thus to join LM_NET, a school librarian or teacher anywhere in the world can send a message to **listserv@listserv.syr.edu**, including in the message box

SUBSCRIBE LM_NET [first name][last name]

(e.g. SUBSCRIBE LM_NET James Herring). The listserv then replies and accepts the new member, and provides an outline of how to send and receive messages from the listserv. A study of LM_NET by Clyde examines the worldwide scope of this listserv and identifies its uses and content. Clyde cites Eisenberg and Milbury, the owners of LM_NET, who outline its advantages as follows: LMNET

> overcomes isolation, by linking even the most remote library media specialist [school librarian] to colleagues throughout the world...
> brings practice into the classroom of library media training programs...
> develops technology skills among library media specialists ...
> provides a sense of belonging. Library media professionals ... have 'a home on the Internet' that is targeted specifically at their interests ...
> puts the library media profession into the center of the national networking movement.[4]

OZTL_NET

In Australia, the listserv for school librarians is OZTL_NET and works on the same basis as LM_NET. To join OZTL_NET, school librarians and teachers can send an e-mail to: **OZTL_NET-request@list-serv.csu.edu**. In the subject line, type **subscribe**. The message field should be left blank and any internet signature should be turned off. Figure 2.3 shows an example of an OZTL_NET list of messages. This is in the form of a digest: the listserv member does not receive all the individual messages in full but receives a list of messages with only the sender's name and the subject included. This allows the busy professional the opportunity to scan the message list and select only those messages that s/he thinks will be relevant. Listserv members are encouraged to be as specific as possible in their subject boxes. If the school librarian chose to read the sixth message, she would click on the message; Figure 2.4 shows the content of that message. This is a good example of the exchange of professional information: this message acted as a stimulation to an online debate about the use of the Internet in schools. The fact that OZTL_NET is based in Australia is

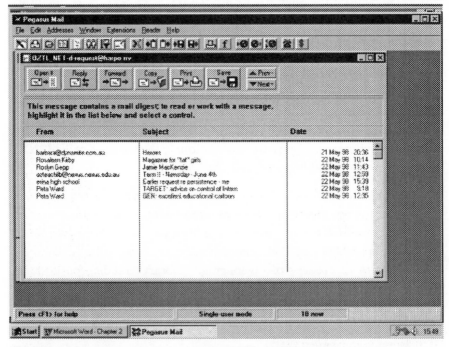

Fig. 2.3 *List of messages sent to the OZTL_NET listserv*

irrelevant in that its membership covers many countries in the world. What is clear is that the debates about issues relating to school libraries, including Internet use, are international. The message in Figure 2.4 was sent from South Africa and was followed by comments from Australia, Canada and the UK.

Hits

The participation in a listserv can be very stimulating for a school librarian in extending her contacts with fellow professionals and can also be a method of saving time through the sharing of resources. In many cases, a listserv member will pose a question on resources to the list, a number of listserv members will reply and the person posing the question will then post a 'hit' to the listserv. This 'hit' represents all (or a summary of all) the messages sent about that topic. Figure 2.5 shows an example of a hit in response to a query on creating and maintaining school websites.

From a school librarian's point of view, being on a listserv provides another source of information on professional issues, and it can also be

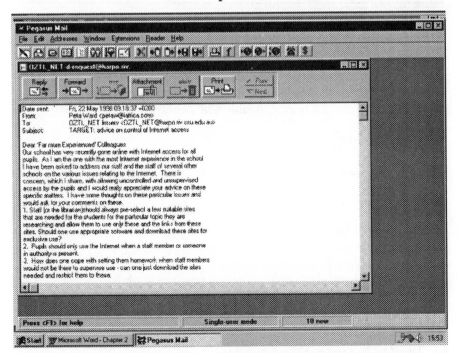

Fig. 2.4   *Request for professional information on the OZTL_NET listserv*

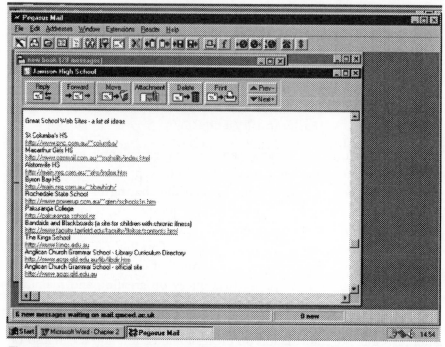

Fig. 2.5   *An OZTL_NET 'hit' on creating school websites*

used to satisfy queries from teachers or pupils – schools in a particular country may share the same curriculum and the same queries may arise in different schools. Some topics, such as acid rain, population control or historical events, will be universal and material found (e.g. on a website) may be useful in different countries.

The World Wide Web

There have been many descriptions of the Web such as Johnstone's 'enormous library of educational information',[5] that try to encapsulate the vast array of different types of information ideas available. Information on the Web is found by connecting to a website, which is a collection of on-screen pages of information. Within each page, there will be hyperlinks to other pages (or other sites) that will provide the reader with more information on a particular topic. Web pages contain information in a variety of formats – text, graphic, photographic, sound, video and animation – depending on the sophistication of the website design. Cunningham et al. describe the Web as 'an exciting, dynamic and rapidly expanding use of the Internet', but warn that although the Web is 'flashy and exciting', a number of problems exist in relation to its use, such as suitability of websites for education and the authority of particular websites.[6] Evaluation of websites is a key element in schools' use of the Web and is dealt with below.

There are many introductions to the Web on the Web itself, and school librarians and teachers wishing in-depth information about the Web can consult sites such as *The online netskills interactive course* at **http://www.netskills.ac.uk/TONIC/**. Access to websites is gained by entering the URL in the location line of an Internet browser such as Netscape Navigator. The URL is made up of different elements. For example, the BBC website address or URL is **http://www.bbc.co.uk**. The 'http://' tells the computer that a Web connection is being made; 'www' indicates that it is a World Wide Web address; and 'bbc.co.uk' shows that the BBC is a company in the UK. Also, 'bbc.co.uk' is the location of the BBC's webserver, which is part of the BBC's computer systems dealing with the Internet. The Web basically works because all websites are either linked to another website or can be found by using a search facility.

Search engines

A search engine is a computer program that allows a user to search for information on the Web. A number of companies worldwide have sought to index the Web and to allow the user to search the multiplicity of websites by entering keywords and using Boolean logic. These companies earn money through advertising, which users see when using their search engine, such as Infoseek, AltaVista, Lycos or Excite. Notess states that users can search using a single search tool, such as those listed above: 'Using a single search engine has the definite advantage of being able to exploit all of that search engine's best features. Infoseek's follow up search, truncation in AltaVista, page depth limits on Hotbot, and Excite's sort options are all examples of important search features when using a single search tool'.[7]

Using a single search engine such as AltaVista provides the user with a choice of a simple or advanced search. (See Figure 2.6 for an example of a search in AltaVista.) In the advanced search option, the user can include a date limit, a language limit and truncation. By using truncation, the school librarian or teacher doing a search can enter part of a keyword and add an asterisk, e.g. pollut*, and the search engine will

Fig. 2.6 *Searching for information on acid rain using the AltaVista search engine*

find material related to a range of aspects of pollution. The key disadvantage of using a single search engine is that the user is limited to searching the database of that particular engine. It is sometimes assumed that all search engines search all of the Web but this is not the case: conducting the same search using AltaVista and Excite will not produce the same results. In terms of searching for material for pupils to use or to support classroom teaching, using one search engine will probably produce relevant sources of information.

Megasearch engines

If the school librarian or teacher wishes to do a deeper search of the Web, then using a multiple search engine or megasearch engine can be more useful and produce better results. Megasearch engines send the user's query to a number of search engines and present the results to the user. Notess states some of the advantages of using such search engines: 'Their capabilities for sorting results by host, keyword, date or search engine can make a long list of results much easier to browse and more informative. Instead of presenting just ten results at a time, the megasearch engines list more hits on a single page which also makes browsing the answer set easier.'8

One megasearch engine used by school librarians around the world is Dogpile. This engine displays which single search engines have been accessed and is very useful for searches using Boolean logic and phrase searching. Figure 2.7 shows an example of a Dogpile search.

Evaluation of websites

The use of information resources in schools has always included an element of evaluation. With sources such as books, school librarians and teachers have identified a range of criteria for selecting books for use in the classroom and/or in the school library. Pupils have also been taught how to use a range of criteria when evaluating the sources they use e.g. pupils doing environmental studies will be taught to distinguish

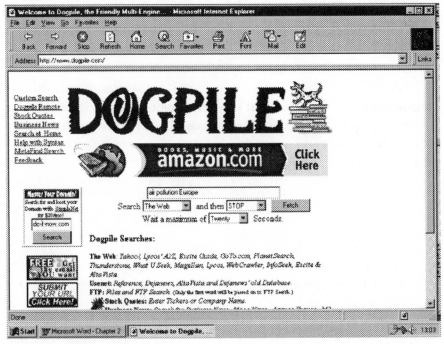

Fig. 2.7 *Searching for information on air pollution using the Dogpile mega-search engine*

between objectively written articles on topics such as transport and reports that may be less objective, such as those written by government officials or by protest groups. The new information resources available on the Web offer schools a much wider variety of information and ideas than print sources and also a greater quantity of sources. However, variety and quantity are not the most important criteria to use when evaluating educational information resources. Evaluation of both print and electronic sources must be related to quality and relevance to the school curriculum. When dealing with print resources, school librarians and teachers are faced with a daunting task in judging the quality of new books, reports or journal articles but, to a certain extent, there is a limited amount of information available, and publishers' catalogues and reviews make the evaluation of material easier. With websites the task is much harder because their quality varies hugely, and there is much less help available to school librarians and teachers in the form of reviews. Thus having an agreed range of criteria for evaluating websites in a school should be a key element of any school's Internet policy. Fortunately for school staff there are a number of excellent guides to assist in identifying criteria, but each school should try to adapt such criteria to its own needs.

Evaluation criteria

Alexander and Tate argue that the existence of websites presents new challenges to educators in the evaluation of information resources. They state that criteria applied to print resources can also be used to evaluate websites, and identify the criteria as:

- Accuracy – How reliable and free from error is the information?
- Authority – What are the author's qualifications for writing on this subject?
- Objectivity – Is the information presented with a minimum of bias?
- Currency – Is the content of the work up to date?
- Coverage – What are the topics included in the work?[9]

The authors add that websites pose additional challenges for school librarians and teachers because of the different nature of websites, and point out the need to identify:

✔ 'marketing-oriented' websites and to distinguish between information and advertising, which is likely to contain some bias

✔ 'infommercial' websites, which blend entertainment, information and advertising and which may also be biased

✔ the use of links to other websites as the quality of linked websites may be much less than the original website

✔ whether additional software is needed to gain full access to a website as this may limit how much information can be gained

✔ 'the instability of web pages', since some websites can either move or disappear or be altered in a way that makes them less suitable.[10]

Evaluation checklist

Harris presents a checklist for evaluating websites, entitled CARS, and provides the following summary, which includes goals for the school librarian, teacher or pupil to aim for:

- **Credibility** – trustworthy source, author's credentials, evidence of quality control, known or respected authority, organizational support. **Goal**: an authoritative source, a source that supplies some good evidence that allows you to trust it

- **Accuracy** – up to date, factual, detailed, exact, comprehensive, audience and purpose reflect intentions of completeness and accuracy. **Goal**: a source that is correct today (not yesterday), a source that gives the whole truth

- **Reasonableness** – fair, balanced, objective, reasoned, no conflict of interest, absence of fallacies or slanted tone. **Goal**: a source that engages the subject thoughtfully and reasonably, concerned with the truth

- **Support** : listed sources, contact information, available corroboration, claims supported, documentation supplied. **Goal**: a source that provides convincing evidence for the claims made, a source that you can triangulate (find at least two other sources that support it).[11]

Harris's checklist can be a useful guide for pupils, though some of the language may have to be adapted to the individual school. It could certainly be used as a starting point for discussion with senior pupils using the Web for individual research projects.

The BBC's free journal *Computers don't bite teachers* also provides a checklist for evaluating websites and gives a list of sites that might be used to test the criteria. The checklist covers the following aspects:

- **1. Audience and purpose** – Who and what is the website for? Is the audience for the site clearly stated or obvious?
- **2. Management** – . . . One of the first things you should look for is to see when the site was last updated. Many of the best sites are updated on a daily basis.
- **3. Ease of use** – A good site should be easy to use. An index is helpful and makes navigation much easier. Check to see if the site has one.
- **4. Content** – How appropriate is the content in terms of curriculum relevance, language level of text, usefulness of graphics . . . usefulness of other media elements. How good is the information and who are the authors?
- **5. Links** – Hotlinks to other pages and sites are important. How relevant are the hotlinks and do they lead on to other useful information?
- **6. Design** – A well designed site will make it obvious how you use it. You should understand the structure and where you are in the website. Simple design and layout are often the most effective . . . The site should also be relatively quick to download.
- **7. Interactive features** – . . . What level of interactivity does the site allow? . . . **very high** – encouraging active participation through communication of answers to tasks; communication is actively encouraged . . .
- **8. Advertising** – Is the site full of 'in your face' advertising that has no relevance to you?
- **9. Unique to Web** – Ask yourself 'Could I do this task or get this information from another source more quickly or more effectively?' If the answer is 'Yes', use the alternative source.
- **10. Recommendation** – The bottom line – would you personally feel confident to recommend the site to a friend, teacher, or colleague as reference or for use with students?[12]

Ranking criteria

As can be seen above, the criteria for evaluating websites can be very extensive. In addition to the criteria already cited, technical elements such as the use of colour, the layout of pages, the availability of help on screen and the sequencing of information on the website can be considered. School librarians and teachers will seek to rank the criteria in terms of importance to themselves and to their pupils: the key criteria for a website must be whether it is relevant to the curriculum and whether the language used is suitable for the intended audience. For example, many university departments around the world have produced excellent websites related to topics within the school curriculum, e.g. volcanoes. However, while a website on volcanoes may be relevant to the curriculum in theory, in practice the level of language used (e.g. the scientific terminology included) may make this site unusable if the intended users are 13-year old pupils whose knowledge of scientific terminology is limited. School librarians and teachers will also teach their pupils, as part of the pupils' information skills programme, how to evaluate the different kinds of information and ideas that they find when using websites, as well as advising the pupils that Web-based information is not necessarily more current or more useful than print sources.[13]

Downloading websites

One way of adding to the school library's range of resources that are available without going online to the Web is to download sites using software such as Webwhacker.[14] Schools can use this type of software to download sites and the links within a site. The advantage of doing this is that sites can be selected by the school librarian and the teacher, with a view to using the site in a particular part of the curriculum. The site can then be integrated into the resource portfolio of the topic along with other resources in the library such as books, CD-ROMs and journal articles. In Linlithgow Academy in Scotland, this was successfully done by the school librarian and a geography teacher who worked together with a secondary year 2 class who were studying the topic of rainforests.

The key elements in the effective use of downloaded sites include the acknowledgement of copyright, i.e. permission to use the site should be granted by the site owner, the guidance given to the pupils in using the site with other sources of information; and a check on the currency of the site where this is important. Software that downloads sites can also be used to produce new versions of the site when the site has been altered. In many schools, sites are downloaded for specific periods of time, made available on the school network and then discarded. Hanson states that while software such as Webwhacker provides a solution to practical issues of access and reliability, it should not be seen as a substitute for online searching by pupils.[15]

Downloading issues

Recent discussions on the use of Webwhacker and downloading in general have taken place on both LM_NET and OZTL_NET and there are differences of opinion. Some school librarians favour Webwhacker, citing its usefulness for demonstrations and also for use with pupils who do not have to go online to find relevant material. These librarians note the copyright issues and make every effort to gain permission before using the sites. Those who do not wish to download websites are particularly concerned about the copyright issues and also whether downloading a site might threaten the existence of that site if it was only ever used offline. Another argument against downloading is that if pupils only use downloaded sites chosen by the teacher or school librarian, they will not get the benefit of searching for their own material and this will restrict their use of the Web. The issue of using downloaded websites (even with permission) will continue to be debated but it can be argued that acquiring downloaded websites and adding them to the stock of the school library is an excellent way of increasing the range of materials available to pupils.

Copyright and the Web

The issue of copyright on the Web is similar to that relating to print material but the nature of Web based information resources highlights a number of key issues. As seen above, the issue of downloading websites is very topical and as technology and software develop it is likely to be much easier to download websites in the future. The key topic is related to ownership and intellectual property rights. If a school downloads all or part of a website, it could be breaching copyright if the author's permission has not been gained. However, a further complication is that even if the school receives permission from the author, how does the school know whether the website itself contains material that breaks copyright law? If a site contains a commercial graphic such as a company logo or a scanned picture of a famous person such as a musician, it may be breaching copyright. Several large multinational companies such as Coca-Cola maintain a watch on websites to ensure that their logos or pictures of their products are only used with permission and/or following a payment to the company. The copyright website[16] is a useful source of guidance both for school librarians and teachers who are using Web material for their own work and for pupils, who may not realize that the use of downloaded Web information or graphics in their coursework may be restricted or even illegal.

Acceptable use policies

The issue of 'responsible' use of the Web is one faced by all schools, and there is a clear dilemma for schools wishing to provide as much access to information as possible for pupils but also wishing to protect them from unacceptable material. Many schools now have acceptable use policies (AUPs), which are agreements between the pupil and the school about the use of the Internet. The AUP stipulates that pupils must not knowingly visit unacceptable sites (e.g. sexist, pornographic, racist, propagandist). The AUP is signed by the pupil and parent/guardian, and access to the Internet can be withdrawn for breaches of the agreement. Examples of AUPs can be found on many school homepages. Defining what constitutes 'acceptable' use may be difficult: anecdotal evidence suggests that teachers and school librarians are more concerned about the amount of time pupils spend searching music or sporting sites than officially unacceptable sites.

Listserv hit on AUPs

A recent 'hit' on AUPs was listed on the OZTL_NET listserv. It included the following:

> The AUP developed at my school began by consulting the students as to what they thought were acceptable/unacceptable uses of the Internet. We compiled a list of these, and wrote a draft policy around it, with penalties for breaking the agreement. The draft was discussed at the next full staff meeting, amendments made, then this was taken to the

P&F meeting for discussion, explanation and amendment. The policy then went back to each class for comment and agreement. Accompanying this, is a procedure for use of the Internet which requires students to complete a proforma planning their session before accessing the Internet. All of these sheets are kept, and become useful data on students' usage, search terms and URL's.[17]

A number of Internet sites were noted where acceptable use policies can be seen, such as **http://www.erehwon.com/k12aup/** (including templates) and the Internet Advocate, a Web-based resource guide for librarians and educators interested in providing youth access to the net, at **http://www.monroe.lib.in.us/~lchampel/ netadv.html**. Figure 2.8 shows an example of an AUP.

Leith Academy Internet Agreement

- I understand that it is strictly forbidden to explore any area of the Internet which is not of legitimate educational value
- Anyone using the system will be subject to having their searches monitored and I expressly consent to such monitoring of my work
- I accept that if there is any doubt about whether a subject is acceptable, it is my duty to check with the supervising member of staff
- I also understand that using the Internet to explore topics or engage in discussions which are inappropriate to a school environment will be considered a serious breach of school discipline
- I realise that no single student can be allowed to 'hog' the system and therefore deny access to others
- I agree to complete a training course before I have any access to the Internet.

The use of the Internet is a privilege, not a right, and any inappropriate use will result in a withdrawal of that privilege and may result in further disciplinary action. The staff of the school will decide what is inappropriate and their decision is final.

Signature of parent or guardian _____ Date_____

Signature of student _____

Training successfully completed on _____

Signature _____

Resource Centre Manager

Fig. 2.8   *Acceptable use policy used in Leith Academy, Edinburgh, Scotland*

Internet projects related to schools

There have been a large number of Internet projects in the UK and elsewhere. School librarians and teachers can learn from these projects by studying examples of good practice in other schools, and in turn avoid some of their mistakes.

The Education Department's superhighways initiative

This initiative covered a number of projects in England, Wales and Scotland that examined the potential use of ICTs in schools and FE colleges and, in many of the projects, schools' use of the Internet in particular. The projects sought to explore the potential of the 'information superhighway' for improving learning in schools, and focused on three main areas:

- Which forms of ICT produce benefits that directly or indirectly improve learning?
- What conditions are needed in a given school or college to enable these benefits to be achieved?
- What infrastructure is needed (locally and nationally) to ensure steady and continuous improvement both in ICT and in the capacity of all schools and colleges to make good use of it?[18]

The project identified six main benefits for the learning process in schools:

- improved subject learning
- the development of network literacy
- improved vocational training
- improved motivation and attitudes to learning
- the development of independent learning and research skills
- social development.[19]

The project report defines network literacy as the pupil's ability to access and create learning resources via networks and to use this access to communicate with other pupils and with teachers. The report argues that 'These three elements of network literacy can be seen as complex extensions of the traditional skills of reading, writing, speaking and listening. The notion also extends previous conceptions of IT literacy, which conventionally involve interactions with and around the computer. To this we must now add interactions at a distance through ICT.'[20] This confirms the view (expanded on in the next chapter) that pupils will need to have sophisticated information skills if they are to exploit Internet resources to good effect.

SchoolNet 2000

This project, which began in September 1998, claims to be the largest educational project ever to be launched in the UK. It is funded mainly by the supermarket chain Tesco. The project will feature input from pupils across the country, who will contribute to building a nationwide picture of life in the UK in the late twentieth century. Pupils will also take part in the project's 'curriculum investigations', in which they will study their own communities from historical, geographical, environmental and other viewpoints and 'tell the world what they learn in their own words'. The project will also fund advisory teachers and Internet centres, and will feature strongly in the Millennium Dome at Greenwich.[21]

Schools Online 2

The second phase of the successful Schools Online project began in 1997. It seeks to 'offer school students a positive, creative role – not just looking at 'interesting stuff' on the World Wide Web, but participating in projects, collaborating and creating material'.[22] The project attempts to extend the potential of pupils and teachers as active participants in the Web and not merely observers; this is done through project ideas relating to the creation of schools' Web pages based on pupils' curricular work. There are also opportunities for teachers and school librarians to comment on activities and establish contacts and joint projects with other schools. Figure 2.9 shows information about the science project within Schools Online 2.

Learning in the New Millennium

This project, like the two previous projects, is coordinated by Ultralab at Anglia University and seeks to bring together schools, scientists and engineers from the Nortel company and researchers in learning technology at Ultralab. The focus of the project, now in phase 2, is based on 'enhancing broad science and technology learning objectives'.[23]

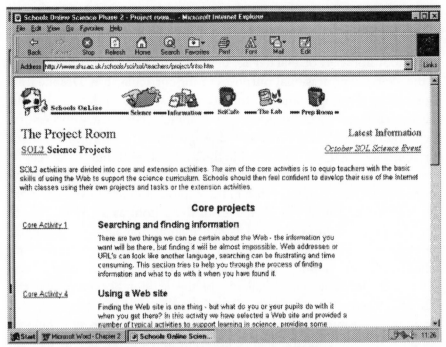

Fig. 2.9   *Information on science projects in Schools Online 2*

British Educational and Communications Technology Agency (BECTa) projects

BECTa undertakes a number of projects funded by the UK government and commercial companies. These include the Educational Internet Service Providers Project, which aims to disseminate examples of good practice found in schools using the Internet for curricular purposes. Using the project website, teachers and school librarians are able to review the work done in other schools and adapt examples of good practice within their own school. Other projects of interest to schools are Netd@ys Europe 1998; Lingu@net, a virtual language centre; Multimedia Portables for Teachers, which reports on how teachers might use portable PCs to aid professional development; and TRENDS (Training Educators through Networked and Distributed Systems), which examines the potential of IT to support teachers' professional development.[24]

Conclusion

The Internet is developing constantly; it is impossible for any individual school librarian or teacher to keep abreast of all the possible uses of the Web for professional purposes or for curricular use. Despite this, by realizing the importance of the need to keep up to date and to do this by participating in listservs or by scanning particular websites that have information on educational developments and projects, school librarians and teachers can provide their schools with new resources in the form of websites, new information from other schools and fellow professionals, and new expertise in the exploitation of the Web to meet the learning and teaching objectives of the school as a whole. School librarians have a particular role as information manager in the school: part of the modern school librarian's job is to make their users – all school staff and pupils – aware of what information resources, both print and electronic, are available in the school library or via the school's Internet connections. Demonstrating a knowledge of and expertise in using the Web for curricular purposes can also help to enhance the status of the school librarian and enable her to play an even more important role in curriculum development than in the past.

References

1   Hahn, H., 'The complete Internet reference', in *Relay business systems: Internet for schools*, Bath, Relay Business Systems, 1998.
2   Winship, I. and McNab, A., *The student's guide to the Internet*, 1998–99 edition, London, Library Association Publishing, 1998.
3   *Computers don't bite*, January 1998, 26.
4   Clyde, L., *School libraries and the electronic community*, Lanham, MD, Scarecrow, 1997.
5   Johnstone, S., 'The plans for ITL in education', in *Internet magazine in education*, Jan 1998 (special BETT edition), 12–13.
6   Cunningham, M. et al., *Schools in cyberspace*, Sevenoaks, Hodder and Stoughton, 1997.
7   Notess, G., 'Towards more comprehensive web searching', *Online*, March/April 1998, 74–6.
8   ibid.
9   Alexander, J. and Tate, M., *The Web as a research tool: evaluation techniques*, 1998. Website:

http://www.science.widener.edu/~withers/evalout
10 ibid.
11 Harris, R., *Evaluating Internet research sources*, 1998. Website:
    http://www.sccu.edu/faculty/R_Harris/evalu8it.htm
12 *Computers don't bite teachers*, 1998, 50–1.
13 Useful Web sources relating to the evaluation of websites include:
    Bibliography on evaluating internet resources:
    http://refserver.lib.vt.edu/libinst/critTHINK.HTM
    Evaluating Web sites for educational uses: bibliography and checklist:
    http://www.iat.unc.edu/guides/irg-49.html
    Teaching critical evaluation skills for world wide web resources (a set of
    checklists to help users analyse the quality of the information on
    websites):
    http://www.science.widener.edu/~withers/webeval.htm
    Internet resource validation project how to evaluate web pages:
    http://www.stemnet.nf.ca/Curriculum/Validate/vali-
    date.html
    Guidelines for evaluating internet information:
    http://info.wlu.ca/~wwwlib/libguides/internet/eval.
    html
    Evaluating internet resources: a checklist:
    http://library.berkeley.edu:8000/bkmk/select.html
    Criteria for evaluating information resources:
    http://www-lib.usc.edu/Info/Sci/pubs/criteval.html
    Critical evaluation surveys for internet resources (a series of evalu-
    ation surveys, one each at the elementary, middle, and secondary
    school levels; also links to many other evaluation resources):
    http://www.capecod.net/schrockguide/eval.htm
    Selection policy for resources and evaluation criteria rating system
    for websites from AASL:
    http://www.ala.org/ICONN/curricu2.html
    Critical thinking and internet resources, including WWW cyber-
    guide ratings for content evaluation, teaching critical evaluation
    skills for www resources, evaluating quality on the net, thinking crit-
    ically about WWW resources:
    http://www.mcrel.org/connect/plus/critical.html

Web site evaluation: a collection of research papers and surveys with links providing criteria that can be used to make judgments about educational websites in K-12 and higher education contexts: **http://web.syr.edu/~maeltigi/Research/RIGHT.HTM**
National school network site evaluation: this feedback form is designed for educators to provide comments regarding their satisfaction with Web sites on levels of educational value and design qualities. Instructions for review and listing of sites requesting reviews are included on linked pages. Whether you use it for submitting a real website or not, it gives some good points to think about when evaluating a site:
http://nsn.bbn.com/webeval/form1.htm
Links to additional sites with web evaluation materials, Widener University/Wolfgram Memorial Library. This page provides several links to sites with articles and guidelines on evaluating Internet resources:
http://www.science.widener.edu/~withers/cklstlnk.htm
Evaluating websites: information on performance related to design, benefits of course websites, design issues:
http://trochim.human.cornell.edu/webeval/webeval.htm
Web site evaluation guidelines from Ed's oasis:
http://www.edsoasis.org/Guidelines.html (this information received from a message to OZTL_NET by Gerald Brown).

14 For further information on Webwhacker, see
http://www.benchin.com/$index.wcgi/prod/1122553

15 Hanson, K., WebWhacking? Issues for an Internet paradigm. In press.

16 The Copyright website is at:
http://www.benedict.com.

17 Message to OZTL_NET from Joy Wilkinson, November 1997.

18 Department for Education and Employment, *Preparing for the information age*, DfEE, 1997. Also available at:
http://www.open.gov.uk/dfee/dfeehome.htm

19 ibid.

20 ibid.

21 For more information on SchoolNet 2000, see
http://www.babelfish.ultralab.anglia.ac.uk/pages/tesco/

22 For more information on Schools Online 2, see:
    http://sol2.ultralab.anglia.ac.uk/
23 For more information on Learning in the New Millennium, see:
    http://research.ultalab.ac.uk/
24 For more information on BECTa projects, see:
    http://www.becta.org.uk

Chapter 3
Information skills and the Internet

After reading this chapter, you will be able to:

✔ **evaluate a range of information skills models**
✔ **understand the interrelated nature of information skills in the PLUS model**
✔ **apply the concepts of information skills to the use of the Internet in schools**
✔ **learn new approaches to information skills and Internet use from the examples provided.**

Developments in electronic information resources

In the modern secondary school, because of developments in technology, pupils are now able to access information in a wide range of formats – print, video, electronic text and multimedia. The *amount* of information that pupils can access has vastly increased in recent years because of the widespread use of CD-ROMs, the use of electronic full-text commercial sources such as Reuters in some schools, and the increasing use of the Internet as an information resource.

Before the introduction of this new technology, it was argued strongly by this author and others cited below that pupils needed to acquire a range of skills in identifying the purpose, location and effective use of concepts, ideas and information in the learning process at school. The information skills needed by pupils when using printed texts such as books, newspapers and periodicals were highlighted and it was shown that pupils' work benefited from a rational and logical approach to information use. The introduction of new technology implies that there is an even greater need for pupils to have skills in identifying their own information needs and making use of effective reading, note-taking, writing and communication skills. Even before the first CD-ROMs appeared in schools, some pupils were asked to make extensive use of video material when researching topics and this introduced concepts of audiovisual literacy, i.e. the skills needed to 'read' a video, take notes from that video in relation to what was seen and heard and use these notes as the basis of an essay or assignment. The use of CD-ROMs, full-text databases and the Internet has reinforced the need for such skills and has highlighted the need for pupils to be much more selective with regard to the information that they find after searching a CD-ROM or a website. This chapter will examine a range of information skills models, including the author's own PLUS model; approaches to the teaching of information skills in schools; the implications of such models for Internet use by pupils; and current practice in schools in teaching information skills to pupils who make use of electronic information resources.

Information skills models

Since the early 1980s a number of models for teaching information skills have emerged from different parts of the world. There are many similarities in the models and school librarians will benefit from studying these and perhaps choosing the elements that are most appropriate for their own school. In this author's experience, no two schools teach information skills in exactly the same way or use exactly the same terminology. All the models view information skills as key learning skills that pupils need to acquire in order to be effective learners. Also, all the models assume that skills will be taught *both* in the classroom and in the library, and that teachers and the school librarian will work together to plan and deliver the information skills programme in the school.

Marland's model

One of the key influences on information skills development around the world was the work coordinated in the UK by Marland, which introduced the nine Steps model of information skills. Marland's group identified nine key questions that pupils, teachers and school librarians needed to address. For example, the first question for pupils was 'what do I need to do?', which was equivalent to 'formulate and analyse need'. The questions and their equivalent statements ended with 'what have I achieved?', which asked pupils to evaluate what they had done in a particular assignment. Marland stressed that the nine steps were not necessarily completed in the order of the list of questions and that in some instances pupils might have to repeat some of the questions, e.g. in order to have a clearer picture of what they were trying to achieve.[1]

The Big Six

In the USA, Eisenberg and Berkovitz's Big Six model identifies six key skills that pupils need, which range from 'Task definition – determine exactly what the information problem is' through to 'Evaluation – determine how effectively and efficiently the information problem solving process was conducted'. Eisenberg's model has been widely adopted in North America and elsewhere, and posters, videos and training sessions are available.[2]

Kuhlthau's model

Another influential model that has emerged from the USA is the work done by Kuhlthau, whose model seeks to identify not only the key elements of the information skills process but the feelings of the pupils while they are engaged in planning and researching assignments. Kulhthau's research shows that pupils' confidence increases the more they find out about their topic, but in the early stages in the process pupils feel much uncertainty about the topic itself and their own approach to the task in hand. Kuhlthau's work is important in that it links both the process and the affective elements of that process. If school librarians and teachers can teach pupils to think about not only what they are doing but also how they feel about what they are doing, then pupils can acquire a range of coping skills when doing an assignment.[3]

The EXIT model

Recent work in the UK by Wray and Lewis has produced the EXIT (Extending Interactions with Texts) model. This contains 'process stages' and 'questions', which range from 'Elicitation of previous knowledge – What do I already know about this subject?' to 'Communicating information – How should I let other people know about this?'. This model puts more stress on reading than do other models, and it is argued that the crucial aspect of the information skills process is the pupils' interaction with the text and 'the construction of meaning in negotiation with the text as written'.[4]

The PLUS model

This author's model of the information skills process is called the PLUS model, which incorporates the elements of Purpose, Location, Use and Self-evaluation. It is designed to use the key elements of previous models while adding emphasis on thinking skills and self-evaluation. The range of skills included in the PLUS model are as follows:

Purpose
- cognitive skills in identifying existing knowledge
- thinking skills such as brainstorming or concept mapping
- skills in identifying information resources.

Location
- locational skills such as the ability to find information in library catalogues, books, journals, CD-ROMs and online information resources
- selection skills in assessing the relevance of information resources
- IT skills in using electronic sources such as the Internet.

Use
- reading skills including the ability to skim and scan information resources to find relevant information or ideas
- interactive skills including the ability to understand the content of what is being read, viewed or listened to and the ability to relate this to existing knowledge
- selective skills including the ability to select the appropriate information and to reject irrelevant information in the context of the purpose identified for using a particular information resource
- evaluation skills including the ability to evaluate information and ideas in relation to aspects such as the currency of the information or ideas, the author and any possible bias in the text
- recording skills including the ability to take notes in a systematic way which relates to understanding and purpose

- synthesizing skills including the ability to bring together related ideas, facts and information about a topic and relating this to existing knowledge
- writing or presentational skills including the ability to write an essay or report or project in a well structured, logically ordered manner which uses the information and ideas found to good effect.

Self-evaluation
- self-evaluation skills including the ability to reflect on the processes involved in assignment-related work and to identify areas of improvement in the effective use of information resources in the future.[5]

Purpose

It is vital that pupils establish a clear purpose when planning and researching an assignment. Identifying a purpose involves pupils in the use of cognitive skills that demand that they think about their existing knowledge of their topic. Pupils can use methods such as brainstorming and concept mapping to explore their topic area, and choose what aspects of that topic they wish to concentrate on. Thus a pupil researching water pollution can think about what has been taught in class about this subject and what s/he knows from his or her own experience. The pupil can then explore the topic via a concept map (e.g. in the form of a spider diagram) to identify the *range* of subtopics, such as the effects of water pollution on industry, on rivers, on the sea and on people's homes. Pupils can then narrow their choice of topic in order to make their assignment more manageable and also to identify keywords relating to their topic. If pupils can successfully establish a clear purpose, then they can proceed to seek information about their topic from a range of resources. If the purpose is not clear, then information seeking will much more problematic.

Location

Pupils have few problems in locating information in the classroom, the school library and elsewhere; locational skills such as the ability to find information in books, journals and CD-ROMs can be seen as fairly mechanical skills. The key aspects of Location relate to selection skills that pupils use to identify relevant information, i.e. information that relates to their purpose. Thus pupils have to select and, importantly, reject information on the basis of whether the information and ideas that they find in information resources are either relevant to their topic or irrelevant.

Use

The Use element of the PLUS model covers a range of skills that pupils will need once they identify relevant information and ideas. Firstly, pupils need to use reading skills, including the ability to skim and scan texts from which they will choose relevant information. In primary schools, pupils are taught reading skills but this often relates mainly to fiction. Work by Millard has shown that reading for information demands different skills from those used when reading fiction and also that, in secondary schools, pupils are often not taught how to read for information.[6] Pupils need to understand what they are reading, viewing or listening to and need to relate this to their existing knowledge. In some cases, pupils may have to go back a stage in the process after they have selected and read relevant sources. For example, reading about a topic may persuade the pupil that his/her actual topic is either too wide or too narrow and s/he may have to return to the Purpose stage in order to define the parameters of the assignment.

Evaluative skills

Pupils also need evaluative skills at this stage so that they can judge the value of the information and ideas that they find in terms of the currency of the information, who the author is and whether there is likely to be any kind of bias in the text being read. This is particularly important when pupils are using the Internet. Pupils then need skills in note-taking so that they take notes on the relevant material they have found but do not fall into the trap of taking too many notes by not rejecting certain sections of the text. Pupils may find that organizing their notes under their keyword headings will relate their notes to their purpose. In organizing their assignment, pupils will need skills in synthesizing information and ideas that they have found and relating this to existing knowledge.

Presentation skills

Finally, in terms of Use, pupils will apply writing or presentational skills. These skills involve the ability to structure an assignment logically, write fluently and coherently, make reference to information sources used in the assignment and construct a bibliography of sources used. Pupils also need to recognize that different methods of presentation may be needed in different contexts, ranging from an academic essay in history to a report in business studies.

Self-evaluation

Pupils need to reflect on their own work and examine the processes through which they went in order to complete the assignment. In some schools, this is built into the assignment specification and pupils are asked whether they might have approached the assignment differently and what they have learned about identifying purpose, location and use of information in the school library and classroom. This is often a difficult aspect for pupils to cope with at first but once they are accustomed to reflecting on their work, they can benefit greatly.

Thus the PLUS model seeks to explore a complex set of interrelated skills that pupils will use and re-use during the completion of an assignment. By asking pupils to take a holistic view of the assignment process and encouraging pupils to reflect on their skills, teachers and school librarians can provide pupils with key learning skills.[7]

Approaches to teaching information skills in schools

A key factor in the success of any information skills programme lies in its integration into the school curriculum. Teaching information skills as a separate 'subject' in the school will not encourage pupils to transfer skills across their curricular subjects. In order to encourage this integration, it is important that school librarians work closely with teachers to ensure that pupils are taught information skills in different parts of the curriculum as well as in the library. In a number of UK schools, school librarians have begun by conducting an information skills audit. In Webster's High School, Angus, Scotland, this took the form of a group of teachers and the school librarian asking all school departments to identify where information skills were taught, examining this audit and producing an 'information skills pilot', which was tested in the geography department to demonstrate how pupils' work could be improved.[8]

The audit involves teachers in different subjects and the school librarian setting down on paper the skills they teach pupils in relation to effective information use. One result of this is likely to be that there are different definitions of information skills and different terminology used. For example, what one teacher calls reference skills, another teacher will call study skills, while the school librarian will refer to information skills. Thus there needs to be agreement on what the skills programme is to be called. If the programme covers the range of information skills outlined above but is entitled 'learning and study skills' as in Glenwood High School, then the school librarian and teachers will not have a problem in using this terminology.

Whole school policy

One of the outcomes of the information skills audit may be a whole school policy on information skills. The key factors that have been identified in relation to whole school information skills policies include the commitment of senior management in the school, cross-professional cooperation, a bottom-up as well as a top-down approach to planning and the commitment of staff to implement the programme across all sections of the school. In some schools, the first steps in the formulation of a policy involve a small group of teachers and the school librarian working together in one area of the curriculum. Once this has been implemented and tested, other groups and senior management become involved in the eventual formation of policy. In many schools, it is the school librarian who has taken the initiative in this area.[9]

Transfer of skills

One of the key problems identified above is the fact that pupils often seem reluctant to transfer skills across curricular subjects. It is therefore important that schools encourage pupils to be aware of applying information skills wherever they are studying, such as in the classroom, the school library or at home. There is often a difficulty in persuading pupils to see the information skills process as an iterative one and not a single process from Purpose to Self-evaluation. School librarians and teachers can therefore work together to remind pupils that when they are working in the classroom, they may be using material that they found in the school library and vice versa. The main aims will be to teach pupils to apply appropriate information skills irrespective of location. One method of doing this is to integrate aspects of information skills into pupil assignments. In many schools, pupils are encouraged to be aware of certain skills, e.g. planning and using concept maps *within* the assignment specification. In some schools, pupils are assessed on the extent to which they can reflect on their own work in a final section in an assignment, which asks them to outline how they completed their assignment and to provide examples, e.g. concept maps, lists of resources used, notes taken etc. and this makes pupils more aware of the importance of the process.[10]

In planning information skills programmes, there is inevitably a heavy load put on the school librarian who will be working with a range of teachers in a common effort to integrate information skills into the curriculum. The key to success in schools lies in the sharing of this load between the school librarian and the teachers, for example, by a number of people taking responsibility for producing parts of any guidelines given to pupils. It may be that the librarian will make a contribution to assignment specifications or go into the classroom to discuss aspects of information retrieval with pupils.

Information skills and the Internet

When applying any of the models referred to above to pupils' use of the Internet, it is clear that there are no completely new learning skills that pupils need to use information and ideas from websites. The IT skills that pupils need will enable them to access the Web, use search engines, make bookmarks and download or save material for future reference. These are skills that will be learned very quickly. One key skill that pupils require when using the Web is the ability to cope with the amount of information and ideas available. This is not a new skill but an extension of a skill pupils first needed when using CD-ROMs (e.g. searching a newspaper such as the *Guardian* on CD-ROM). Because the Internet is not structured in the same way as other electronic information resources, the chances of a pupil retrieving much more information than is needed are greatly increased when the pupil uses a search engine such as Altavista.

Johnson reinforces this point by stating that 'In the past, the researcher's main challenge was to locate enough data to make meaningful use of it. The Internet researcher has the opposite challenge: to select useful data from the glut of information on the networks of 11 million computers'.[11] Eisenberg and Johnson state that, in relation to using the Internet, pupils will acquire computer skills for specific purposes but that computer skills are not necessarily related to effective use of the information and ideas found using these skills. They add that, when using the Internet, 'Students may learn isolated skills and tools but they will still lack an understanding of how these various skills fit together to solve problems and complete tasks.' Eisenberg and Johnson try to identify key applications of information skills when pupils are using the Internet and argue that, in relation to 'task definition', pupils may use e-mail and listservs to communicate with teachers about assignment issues. Pupils may also use e-mail to 'facilitate cooperative activities amongst groups of students locally and globally'. Other skills include the ability to assess the value of Internet resources, locate information on the Web such as library OPACs, commercial databases and government and academic sources by using search engines; and, in terms of communicating information, create webpages using HTML (hypertext markup language).[12]

Libraries of the future project

In the UK, the recently completed 'Libraries of the Future' project examined pupils' use of the Internet and stressed the need for pupils to learn the requisite information skills in order to cope with the range and varying quality of information found on the Web. The project concluded that:

✔ the retrieval skills used in dealing with print resources could be applied to the use of the Web
✔ careful planning of searches was even more important when searching the Web
✔ pupils should be encouraged to use both electronic and print resources when completing assignments and should not value Web resources above print resources

✔ pupils found searching the Web difficult because of the large amounts of sites identified and because of the time it took to find relevant information

✔ much of the information and ideas found on the Web were not suitable for the school curriculum.

The project was encouraged to see that some pupils had developed skills in evaluating information found in websites and that pupils were good at summarizing what was found. The project report argues strongly that pupils needed 'high levels of skills . . . to analyse and synthesise masses of information'.[13]

The PLUS model and Web use

The PLUS model can be used with pupils who find some of the material for assignments or projects by using the Web. Identifying purpose is clearly vital in relation to Web use. If pupils are encouraged to brainstorm with each other about topics and to draw up concept maps of their topic, then they are more likely to be able to construct searches that will provide them with relevant material. Identifying purpose also allows pupils to consider what knowledge and information they already have about a topic, and this may include websites that they have examined in the past or have been encouraged to use by the teacher or school librarian. Locating information on the Web is, as has been seen, very easy but locating *relevant* information often poses problems for pupils. Thus pupils need to learn not only how search engines work but also the best way to construct searches on the Web in order to find material that is useful.

The Use aspect of the PLUS model is where pupils may find most difficulty in applying the skills they have been taught. This is because of the complex nature of the information that they may find on the website. Pupils will have to use skimming and scanning skills immediately following a search in order to identify which websites are potentially useful and which ones are either irrelevant or too academic. Once pupils access the website, their interaction with the text, graphics, photographs and perhaps sound and video will need to be effective if they are to gain new insights and relate these to their existing knowledge.

Reading a website

'Reading' a website involves a range of skills, in particular:

✔ selection of relevant parts of the website and the rejection of other parts
✔ decision as to whether links to other sites should be followed up
✔ evaluation of the information found in terms of authority, level of language, currency of information and possible bias
✔ taking notes related to purpose and avoiding the temptation to copy and paste sections of the website for inclusion in an assignment.

Once websites have been used, pupils will want to integrate material from the Web into their final written or oral presentation. The visual attraction of websites can often lead pupils into an over-valuation of the information found, and teachers and school librarians will stress to pupils that information and ideas found in print materials in the school library or elsewhere may have equal or even more value than Web-based information. The inclusion in a pupil's assignment of a down-loaded webpage may add to the visual attractiveness of the assignment but it may add nothing to the relevance of the content. Given the right guidance in the classroom and the school library, pupils can learn to choose the content of their assignment carefully.

Reflection

In terms of self-evaluation, pupils can be encouraged to reflect on their use of the Web as an information source. In some schools, teachers and school librarians require that pupils include in their assignments not only a bibliography of sources used but a summary of what sources were consulted, what the value of the sources was and whether pupils found using the Web was an aid or a hindrance to finding information related to their purpose. It is this kind of practice that will allow pupils to think clearly about using Web resources for their assignments or projects and also encourage them to learn from previous use of the Web when undertaking new coursework.

Examples from schools

Ripon Grammar School, Yorkshire, England

Ripon Grammar School is an excellent example of a cooperative venture between the school librarian and a range of subject teachers to develop their pupils' information skills further through use of the Web. Pupils are given verbal and written guidance on planning, searching, recording and evaluation. This school bases its information skills programme on the PLUS model. Figure 3.1 shows a handout on *searching* the Web for information but there is a clear emphasis on planning, reading and evaluation as well as searching techniques.

When using the Internet, pupils are provided with a search log which they fill in. The search logs are used to analyse pupils' use of the Web and to add to the school's store of bookmarked sites. Pupils are also given an 'Online research form', which helps them to record the purpose of their search, their existing knowledge of the topic, their choice of keywords and a record of their time spent online. This form includes clear guidance: 'The most successful Internet searches are those which are carefully planned'.

Linlithgow Academy, West Lothian, Scotland

Part of this school's information skills programme is carried out by the school librarian and staff from the English department. It is based around the theme of pirates. Pupils are encouraged to find information about pirates in a variety of information resources in the school library, classroom and outside the school. Part of the programme introduces pupils to the Web. It provides the pupils with simple definitions of aspects of the Web such as URLs and search engines. The pupils are guided towards the websites, one of which is shown in Figure 3.2 and answer a series of questions related to each site. This is followed by exercises in creative writing on the part of the pupils in which they use the ideas and information gained from using the information resources, including the websites, as the basis for stories and poetry.

Methodist Ladies College (Australia)

As part of this school's cross curricular information skills programme, the library homepage on the school's intranet provides a style manual

<u>Internet Search Advice</u>

1. Decide what information you need
Be specific! There is a lot of information out there . . . avoid getting side-tracked by knowing exactly what you want.

2. Know where to look for the information you need
Make a list of strategies . . . what search engines to use, does the school have any bookmarks which might be useful?

3. Select the best resources
Learn to read the 'hit list' quickly, evaluate the URLs and description quickly. Is the site created by a government, company, organization or individual? Do you recognise the sponsor as a reputable source of information? (e.g. Reuters news agency) . . .

4. Find the best information
Skim the entry quickly. Look for clues: is there a date of publication? [Are] the author's name and email address on the page? Is there any information about the sponsor (company, organisation etc.)?
Is there an introduction or contents list to the site that tells you what is included? Is the site user-friendly and easy to read?
Remember: Before you accept ANY information from the Net, you should be able to verify it with a second source. There are no controls over the accuracy or bias of material published on the Net . . . BEWARE!

5. Analyse the information
Does the information answer your original question? Do you need to move on to another hypertext link for more information?

6. Record what you need
How will you use the information that you have found? Do you want to take notes quickly or do you want to save it as a file to print out later offline? (You will not get pictures when you print out offline but printing online can take a long time and you may run out of time before the picture has finished print-ing.)
If this is a good site, should you save it as a bookmark?

7. Evaluate your search offline
Look back at the log and assess the value of your search. Would you have found the same information by using a book or a CD-ROM etc.? Do you think the information you found was biased or inaccurate in any way?
What mistakes did you make and how could you improve your searching in the future?

Fig. 3.1 *Advice on searching the Web in Ripon Grammar School, Yorkshire, England*

which gives pupils guidance on aspects of writing, these are shown in Figure 3.3. This represents a creative use of part of a school website that serves as an online reference point for pupils to use when writing assignments.

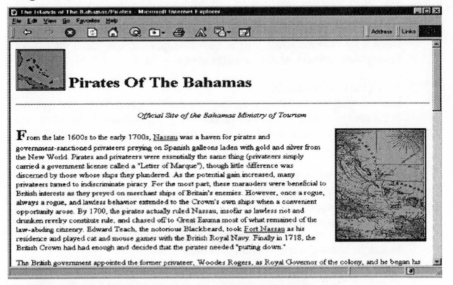

Fig. 3.2 *Website used by pupils in Linlithgow Academy, West Lothian, Scotland in their information skills programme*

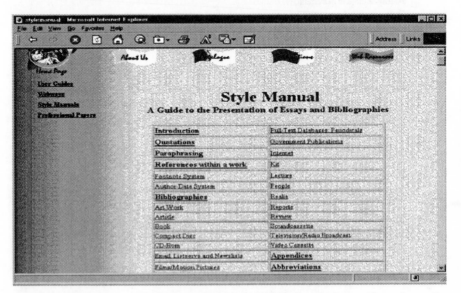

Fig. 3.3 *Advice on writing essays in Methodist Ladies College, Kew, Australia*

References

1 Marland, M. (ed.), *Information skills in the secondary curriculum*, London, Methuen, 1981.
2 Eisenberg, M. and Berkovitz. R., *Information problem solving: the big six approach to library and information skills instruction*, Ablex, 1990. Website:
   http://edweb.sdsu.edu/edfirst/bigsix/basics.html
3 Kuhlthau, C., *Virtual school library*, Libraries Unlimited, 1997.
4 Wray, D. and Lewis, M., *Extending literacy*, London, Routledge, 1997.
5 Herring, J. E., *Teaching information skills in schools*, London, Library Association Publishing, 1996.
6 Millard, E., *Developing readers in the middle years*, Milton Keynes, Open University Press, 1994.
7 Herring, J. E., op. cit.
8 ibid.
9 ibid.
10 ibid.
11 Johnson, D., 'Student access to the Internet', *Emergency librarian*, **22** (3), 1995, 8–12.
12 Eisenberg, M. and Johnson, D., 'Computer skills for information problem solving: learning and teaching technology in context', *ERIC digest*, March 1996.
13 National Council for Educational Technology, *Libraries of the future: final report*, Coventry, NCET, 1996.

Chapter 4
English

Having read this chapter, you will be able to:

✔ **evaluate the use of the Web for providing information resources in English**
✔ **use the example websites within the English curriculum in your school**
✔ **learn from the examples provided about linking print resources and Web resources in English**
✔ **examine the possibility of creating in-school instructional websites for the English curriculum.**

The National Curriculum

The National Curriculum in England and Wales identifies a range of knowledge and skills that pupils will be required to learn in English. Guidelines state that, in relation to reading at Key Stages 3 and 4 (i.e. secondary school), pupils should be taught to:

- extract meaning beyond the literal, explaining how choice of language and style affects implied and explicit meanings;
- analyse and discuss alternative interpretations, unfamiliar vocabulary, ambiguity and hidden meanings;
- analyse and engage with the ideas, themes and language in fiction, non-fiction, drama and poetry.[1]

The National Curriculum also states that:

Pupils should be given opportunities to talk and write about a wide range of reading, learning to articulate informed personal opinions. They should be encouraged to respond, both imaginatively and intellectually, to what they read. Within a broad programme of reading, they should be given opportunities to:

- reflect on the writer's presentation of ideas, the motivation and behaviour of characters, the development of plot and the overall impact of a text;
- distinguish between the attitudes and assumptions displayed by characters and those of the author;
- appreciate the characteristics that distinguish literature of high quality;
- appreciate the significance of texts whose language and ideas have been influential, e.g. Greek myths, the Authorised Version of the Bible, Arthurian legends;
- consider how texts are changed when adapted to different media, e.g. the original text of a Shakespeare play and televised or film versions.[2]

Information resources

In relation to information resources, the guidelines state that:

Pupils should be given opportunities to read factual and informative texts in order to:
- select information;
- compare and synthesise information drawn from different texts, e.g. IT-based sources and printed articles;
- make effective use of information in their own work;
- evaluate how information is presented.

In using information sources, pupils should be taught to sift the relevant from the irrelevant, and to distinguish between fact and opinion, bias and objectivity.[3]

The National Curriculum also provides guidance on the types of literature and other sources that pupils might use – these include novels, plays and poetry as well as non-fiction texts such as autobiographies, journals, diaries and travel writing. Until recently, pupils would study English mainly through texts, though a number of excellent CD-ROMs (e.g. on Shakespeare's plays) are now available. In many schools, school librarians and teachers have been using the Web as a valuable source of ideas and information that pupils can use along with other materials in the school or at home.

The use of the Web to support the English curriculum is directly related to the range of skills outlined above by the National

Curriculum, and the same skills can be found in curricular guidelines for English in many countries. The advantages of using the Web to support the English curriculum are that it can provide pupils with access to resources that would not otherwise be available to them, allow pupils to study English in a different medium, encourage pupils to evaluate the opinions of the authors of the websites used and provide teachers with a range of resources and ideas that can help to enrich their own teaching.

BECTa sources

In the BECTa TRENDS Teaching and Learning with the Internet project, the following sites were assessed in relation to teaching English:

✔ *Exploring English*
   http://www.dsoe.com/explore/english/
✔ *T S Eliot*
   http://www.columbia.edu/acis/bartleby/eliot/index.html
✔ *Seamus Heaney*
   http://sunsite.unc.edu/ipa/heaney/
✔ *Internet public library: the author page*
   http://www.ipl.org/youth/AskAuthor/
✔ *Educational Web adventures*
   http://www.eduweb.com/ss.html
✔ *What the thunder said: T S Eliot*
   http://www.deathclock.com/thunder
✔ *Storyteller sources on the Internet*
   http://users.aol.com/storypage/sources.htm
✔ *Bibliomania: the network library*
   http://www.mk.net/~dt/Bibliomania/index.html
✔ *The human-languages pages*
   http://www.june29.com/HLP/
✔ *Puffin: who's who*
   http://www.puffin.co.uk/Puffin/Authors/
✔ *The Dickens page*
   http://lang.nagoya-u.ac.jp/~matsuoka/Dickens.html
✔ *Virtual seminars for teaching literature*
   http://info.ox.ac.uk/jtap/4

By accessing sources such as the UK's BECTa or SCET (Scottish Council for Educational Technology) sites, school librarians and teachers can find and evaluate sources that have been used by schools and investigate the suitability of the sites for their own use. For example, many schools use the sites hosted by publishers, such as the Puffin site cited above. By accessing this site, the school librarian and teacher can gain more information about the author of particular books that pupils have read or are about to read.

Contact with authors

A number of schools, such as Islington Green School, London, have subsequently made e-mail contact with authors and set up visits to the school by the author. Figure 4.1 shows an example of the school's contact with Ginn authors. This type of contact can greatly enhance the experience of teaching and learning English. Both the school librarian and English teachers at Islington Green School note that the pupils are more motivated and enthusiastic about English as a subject following contact with authors and use of the publisher's site **http://www. ginn.co.uk**

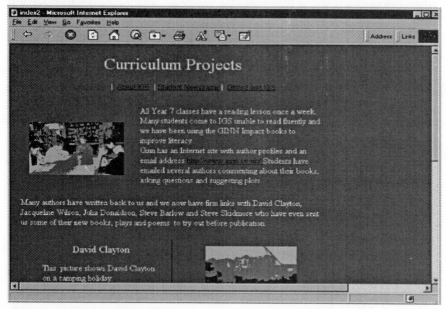

Fig. 4.1 *Contact with an author on the website of Islington Green School, London, England*

Case study: St Mary's School, Johannesburg, South Africa

At this school, in year 2 of secondary school, pupils undertake a series of projects within English, history and drama relating to the theme of protest. As the school is a girls' school, the role of women plays a prominent part in the projects. In English, pupils do work in the areas of protest literature in the form of South African short stories and poetry, and they also produce a newspaper in groups around the theme of the role of women and protest. Pupils are encouraged to use a range of information resources in the classroom and in the school library, and to use the school library's online catalogue to locate resources, e.g. short stories, which will be found at 808.31 on the library shelves. The school librarian (who is also the media teacher) works in advance with teachers to identify both the tasks that the pupils will carry out and information resources in the library and on the Web.

Figure 4.2 shows the guidance given to pupils who choose to do a poetry task.

Poetry tasks

When the pupils find the Bleksem site, they can select a poem to read and have the ability to contact the publishers through the 'respond' option. Figure 4.3 shows the Bleksem webpage. Pupils then complete a second poetry task, outlined in Figure 4.4.

Poems may be found through the online catalogue and at www.africa.cis.co.za at Bleksem, the online SA alternative poetry archive, as well as at www.marques.co.za for Alan Paton's collected poems . . . Choose a South African poem depicting protest or abuse.
a) What is the theme of your poem?
b) Why do you think the poet wrote this poem?
c) Look at the general structure and technique of the poem. Are there any figures of speech or imagery which enhance the message in the poem which the poet is trying to convey? Discuss this in four good sentences.

Fig. 4.2 *Guidance on poetry resources on the Web for pupils in St Mary's School, Johannesburg, South Africa*

Fig. 4.3 *Bleksem poetry website used by pupils in St Mary's School, Johannesburg, South Africa*

You are organizing a campaign against the abuse in your poem:

a) Develop a slogan for your campaign
b) Create a brochure to be handed out to people to make them aware of abuse and what should be done to stop it OR produce a TV advertisement script to persuade viewers against the abuse OR write a newspaper article about the abuse and what should be done to end it. Pin up your work in the Exhibition area for assessment by your colleagues.
c) Load **http://www.africa.cis.co.za** on the Internet and access Za Zoo entertainment and literature and find Barefoot Press's interactive poetry page. Read through some of the examples which have been submitted by South Africans.
d) Send your own sweet, funny and short poem protesting about something in your life. Print the screen and hand in your poem with your other work. Do not forget to check in future whether your poem was chosen for inclusion on the Internet. You may also write to Barefoot Press at barefoot. press@pixie.co.za via e-mail.
e) Why do you think they call themselves Barefoot?

Fig. 4.4 *Poetry task for pupils in St Mary's School, Johannesburg, South Africa*

South African poets

When the pupils access the Barefoot Press website, they are given the option of reading poems by selected South African poets. Figure 4.5 shows the response to choosing Phedi Tlhobolo and Figure 4.6 shows one of the poems by this author.

The poetry task set for the pupils at St Mary's demonstrates how the school librarian and the teachers can make very good use of the Web to allow pupils to access resources not otherwise available to them in other media. One teacher commented, 'The Internet is a wonderful source especially here in South Africa where it is so expensive to import books and our book prices are so high'. The English teachers agreed that the existence of the Web not only allows greater access to information resources, such as the poetry archive, but also serves to extend the curriculum in a number of ways. For example, pupils are not restricted to writing poems that they share with each other: they can interact with website poetry by responding to poems they read and can submit their own work to the publishers online. The staff also agreed that the Web can be very time-consuming to search and very slow to respond at times. Cooperation between the school librarian/media teacher and other staff was important, especially in relation to

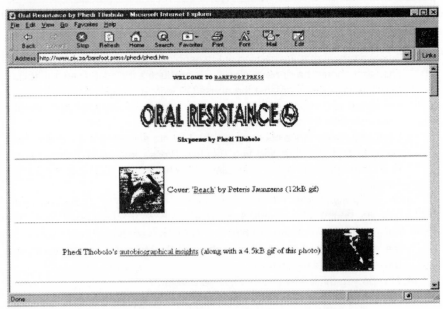

Fig. 4.5 *Example of poets available on the Barefoot Press website*

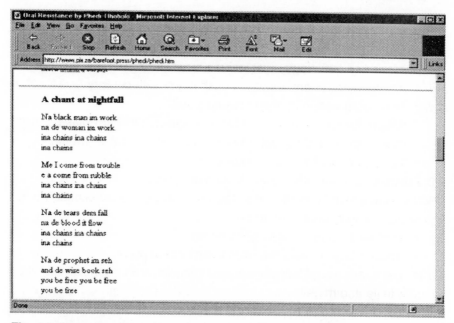

Fig. 4.6 *Example of a poem used by pupils in St Mary's School, Johannesburg, South Africa*

identifying sites for pupils to search in advance and bookmarking these sites for easy access by pupils. Although it could be argued that this restricts the pupils' access to resources, in practical terms identifying sites for pupils helps to focus the pupils' attention on the task in hand and enables pupils to find websites as quickly as they find books on the library shelves.

Case study: Hallet Cove School, Kangarilla, Australia

The pupils taking English in year 3 of this secondary school are asked to complete an activity that requires each pupil to search for poems on the Web and complete the tasks shown in Figure 4.7.

The pupils are encouraged to search the school library catalogue to find examples from the school's own poetry collection but are also given a list of websites to access, including 'Larrikin's Lair', which contains Australian poetry and an Australian poem of the month. Figure 4.8 shows the choice of poems on offer and Figure 4.9 shows an example poem from this site.

Task

1. Your task is to create a poetry anthology, containing a minimum of ten poems. Your anthology must include the following:
   - An Australian poem about the bush in the 19th century
   - One poem written by the following poets:
     William Wordsworth, Gerard Manley Hopkins, William Blake, Emily Dickinson, T. S. Eliot, John Keats, Elizabeth Barrett Browning
   - Three poems of your own choice
2. Illustrate your anthology and create a title page
3. Select one of the poems and write a short article of approximately one page in length, commenting on:
   - Your reasons for choosing the poem
   - How the poet treated the main theme of the poem
   - The use of poetic language such as similes, metaphors, alliteration, rhyme and rhythm
4. Select one poem to read aloud in the class
5. Write a poem of your own

Extension

Add your poem to the World Wide Web using a site which accepts student work. An example is Kid Pub WWW Publishing at http://www.kid-pub.org/kidpub/

Fig. 4.7 *Poetry assignment for pupils in Hallett Cove School, Kangarilla, Australia*

As with the example from St Mary's above, this case study demonstrates how the Web might serve to help the teacher make a poetry assignment more interesting and more varied for the pupils. The school librarian and English teachers in this school noted an increase in motivation by pupils doing this assignment because of the opportunity to use the Web and to access a site that publishes work done by the pupils themselves. As with other subject areas, there is a danger that pupils will become over dependent on the Web, but by integrating print, audiovisual and electronic resources the school librarian and teachers can ensure that pupils do not see the Web as the only source of poetry material. The poetry anthology example from Hallet Cove School is taken from 'Weblinks', which offers schools a range of websites, lesson plans and curricular ideas.[4]

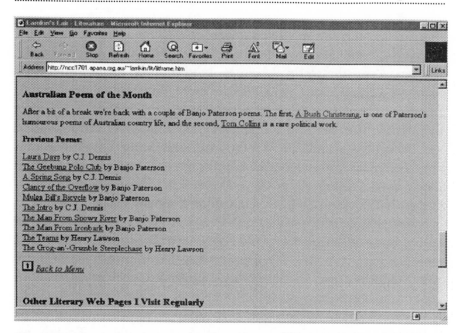

Fig. 4.8 *Poems offered on the Larrikin's Lair website*

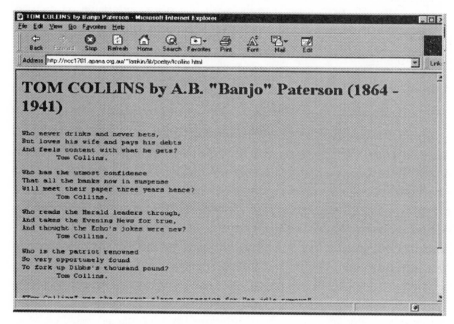

Fig. 4.9 *Example of a poem used by pupils in Hallett Cove School, Kangarilla, Australia*

Conclusion

The above examples show that the Web is a rich resource for English teachers across the world. It can be used to good effect in the classroom and school library to extend the curriculum and motivate pupils. In order to benefit from access to Web resources in English, it is clear that pupils still require skills of thinking, understanding and interpretation, which they would need if they had only printed resources available. Using the Web cannot be seen as the sole resource for teaching pupils how to interpret the ideas they find in a poem - it is important that school librarians and teachers stress to pupils that the Web is an information resource that has to be used with other resources in the school, and that pupils are taught how to evaluate the information and ideas they get from the Web. Despite this caveat, motivation in pupils is an important part of the learning process, and if using the Web makes pupils pay more attention to their subject topic and task, then it is clearly of benefit to both staff and pupils. The National Curriculum guidelines outlined above show that pupils studying English are expected to use a wide range of skills in analysis, interpretation and reflection. By providing pupils with a more extensive choice of resources to use, school librarians and teachers can encourage pupils to put these skills into practice.

References

1   Department for Education and Employment, *The National Curriculum for English*, 1998.
    http://www.dfee.gov.uk/nc/engindex.html
2   ibid.
3   ibid.
4   For more information about Weblinks, see:
    http://www.ozemail.com.au/~pledgerp or e-mail pledgerp@mail.ozemail.com.au

Chapter 5
Science

Having read this chapter, you will be able to:

✔ **evaluate the use of the Web for providing information resources in science**

✔ **evaluate the use of an instructional website for teaching science in your school**

✔ **examine ways in which you can adapt the examples provided here to the needs of your own school**

✔ **identify how you might work with colleagues to exploit Web resources for science in your school.**

The Association for Science Education (ASE)

The ASE review of science teaching for the new millennium includes a number of quotations[1] from experts whose aim is to increase interest in science amongst school pupils and to improve the teaching of science in schools. These include 'Science education must continue to focus on the MAJOR conceptual ideas of science but rid itself of clutter' (Rosemary Feasey, response to ASE Science Education 2000+ initiative); 'In science education there has been a spate of research, which has shown that pupils of all ages who have learnt science well enough to pass traditional examinations show alarming gaps in their understanding of basic ideas' (Paul Black and Wynne Harlen, *Guardian*, 1990); 'How to teach learning', 'School Science is devoid of joy and emotional involvement; a mechanistic model divorced from nature', (Kevin McCarthy, *TES*, 1995); 'A good science education should seek to develop a range of intellectual skills and cognitive patterns which would help youngsters to handle the problems of growing up in, and integrating with, a society that is heavily dependent on scientific and technological knowledge and its utilization', (*Alternatives for science education*, ASE, 1979). The following were also cited:

The major aim of science education is to encourage pupils to think and act as responsible scientists through providing opportunities for them to acquire knowledge and understanding of relevant concepts and through practising the problem-solving and practical skills associated with the scientific process of enquiry. The long-standing debate about the relative importance of knowledge and skills has not been helpful because both are equally important to the scientist *(Effective learning and teaching in Scottish secondary schools: The Sciences*, SOED);

If we can revise our policy on the teaching of science to make the subject more human, more relevant and certainly more fun then we will have educated our children properly. The time for the purist approach is not at key stages 3 and 4 but later. We are so bogged down in teaching the detail of science that the pupils cannot see the wood for the trees (James Williams, in *TES*, 1995);

and

There is also evidence that pupils regard the sciences, and the physical sciences in particular, to be too demanding and to lack either relevance or excitement *(Science and mathematics in schools – a review*, OFSTED).

The ASE also states that:

learners are entitled to use appropriate opportunities to collect, store, retrieve and present scientific information. There should be appropriate progression from being able to use IT, to judging when to use IT to collect, handle and investigate scientific information . . . teachers should be able to evaluate the potential of video-conferencing, email communication and Internet access as tools for learning.[2]

It is clear from the UK's leading association for science teachers that the use of the Web in learning about science can contribute to achieving some of the aims identified in the quotations above, i.e. by making science more interesting and relevant to pupils and, most importantly, by allowing pupils to work more independently than before in pursuing their scientific enquiries. This chapter will examine examples of instructional websites for learning and teaching in science, Web based resources related to science teaching, and the importance of integrating a range of information resources relating to science in schools.

Case study: Ripon Grammar School, Yorkshire, England

Ripon Grammar School is a Local Education Authority selective grammar school at the secondary level. At present, Internet access in the school is limited and there is one Pentium computer in the school library specifically reserved for Internet use. Access to the Internet is provided by Research Machines, which act as the Internet service provider (ISP), using a 28.8 bps modem and analogue telephone connection. There are limited funds for using the Internet, and it is therefore seen as very important that the school librarian and teachers who wish the pupils to use the Web for scientific work plan ahead carefully in order to make maximum use of the time available. The school has its own website and this is available to pupils offline during the school day and online for an hour after school. A significant number of pupils in the school have Internet access at home.

Instructional website[3]

The school librarian and the physics teachers created an instructional web-site for a study programme with both contributing to the text and graphics in the website. The school librarian designed the pages and the hypertext links within the pages using Microsoft's Front Page authoring software (see Chapter 10). One of the key issues relating to the website development was providing pupils with access to a website offline, so that pupils with limited experience of using the Internet or with no access at home could develop skills in using a website and use the Internet in a manner very close to that of a real online session. One aspect of the programme included a discussion amongst the pupils about the content of websites, as it was clear that if the school librarian and teachers in Ripon Grammar School could produce a physics website, then it was possible for others to do so as well. This led to work on the importance of evaluating websites especially in relation to the presentation of scientific evidence.

Programme objectives

The school librarian and the physics teachers worked together to develop a programme of study for year 7 (first level secondary) pupils. The general objectives of this programme were to cover the relevant topics in the physics syllabus in accordance with National Curriculum guidelines and to develop independent research skills and information handling skills amongst the pupils. The school uses the PLUS model across the curriculum to teach information skills, and the physics programme allowed pupils to put the relevant skills into practice while studying physics. The specific objectives of the programme included the study of the topic 'The earth's place in the universe': Figure 5.1 shows the physics programme's homepage.

Within this programme, pupils worked in small groups, completed a series of worksheets, produced a written report of two A4 sides and gave an oral presentation of their findings to the rest of the class. Thus while studying the scientific aspects of the physics syllabus, pupils were also encouraged to develop skills in discussion, cooperation, research, reading, writing and speaking. The website was designed as a tool to provide pupils with further knowledge of physics, to develop pupils' skills in using the Internet, to provide pupils with information research challenges and to link existing information resources with Web resources. The intention was also to make the physics syllabus attractive and interesting for pupils and to

Fig. 5.1 *Physics project homepage on the website of Ripon Grammar School, Yorkshire, England*

increase their motivation to study in this curricular area. Figures 5.2 and 5.3 show parts of the syllabus available to the pupils.

Information resources

In this part of the programme, the pupils were encouraged to view all school information resources as important and in addition to the website and the links to other sites, the pupils used general reference sources in the school library in the form of encyclopedias, dictionaries and guidebooks in both print and CD-ROM format. The pupils also had access to physics books in the school library and to a project box, which included books and other materials relating to the solar system on loan from North Yorkshire's School Library Service's project loan service. This group of resources was used both in the school library and in the physics classroom. Figure 5.4 shows the range of additional information resources available for the programme and Figure 5.5 shows the links to other websites.

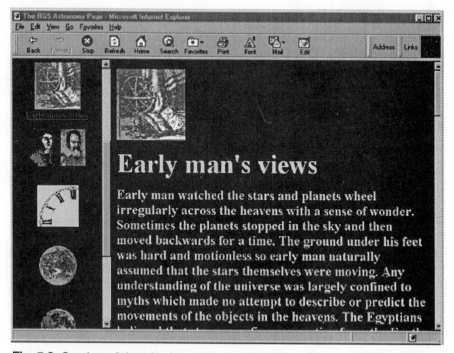

Fig. 5.2 *Section of the physics syllabus for pupils in Ripon Grammar School, Yorkshire, England*

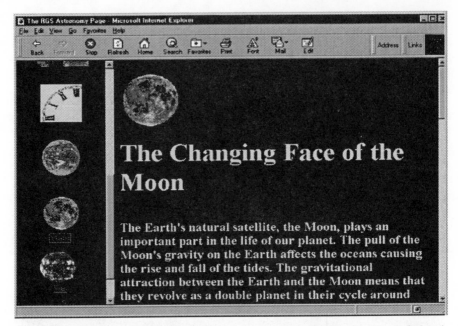

Fig. 5.3 *Section of the physics syllabus for pupils in Ripon Grammar School, Yorkshire, England*

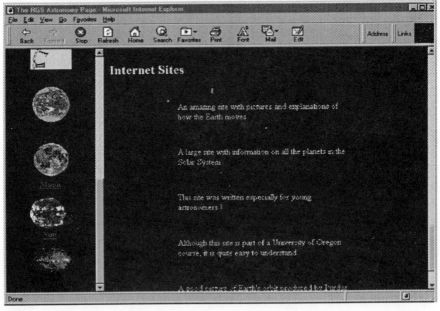

Fig. 5.4   *Additional information resources for physics available to pupils in Ripon Grammar School, Yorkshire, England*

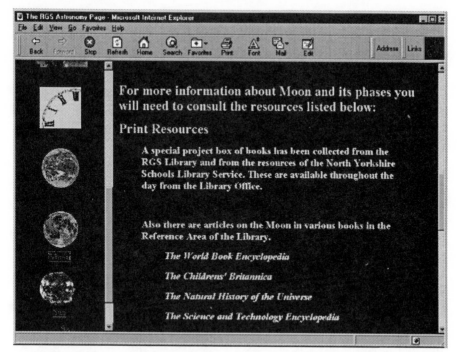

Fig. 5.5 *Links to other physics websites for use by pupils in Ripon Grammar School, Yorkshire, England*

Evaluation of the programme

The programme was very successful and it was felt that the addition of the instructional website and links to other Web resources enhanced the value of the study for the pupils. The physics teachers noted that the groups used the webpages as a catalyst for preliminary discussion about their topic and the potential resources that they could use. The pupils themselves also commented on the value of the webpages in relation to planning their work, as each group could view the webpages together and therefore have equal access to the core information needed. In this school, differentiation is often required to meet the needs of very bright pupils who want to go beyond the general requirements of an assignment: the links on the physics webpages to external astronomical sites provided this differentiated material. These pupils could book online time after school to do further work and those with Internet access at home located and printed out material that could be used by the rest of the group.

In the opinion of the school librarian and the physics teachers, the intro-duction of a new teaching and learning methodology as part of the physics programme provided a new impetus for pupils and teachers alike. They also took the realistic view that it was the *integration* of the website and weblinks with existing resources and existing teaching methods that provided the key to success. The school staff intend to extend the provision of instructional websites and links to external websites through increased provision for Internet access in the school. Their view is that by using the Internet as an internal and external information resource, the curriculum can be supported and enhanced and the pupils' information skills can be developed across the curriculum.

Web resources in science

There is a vast range of websites providing scientific information and instructional websites in the science area, which is *potentially* extremely useful to school librarians and teachers in different countries. However, as with other curricular topics, the usefulness of a particular website, for example on the solar system, may be limited because of the level of language used or the level at which the topic is studied. For example, a website related to a third-year university physics course is not likely to be understood by the year 7 pupils in Ripon Grammar School. Nevertheless, there is an increasing amount of material available that is related to schools and is structured at different levels. The ASE site referred to above includes a useful list of potential links for learning and teaching in science; Figure 5.6 shows a selection of these.

The Busy Teachers' WebSite[4]

An example of a very useful site for school librarians and science teachers is the Busy Teachers' site, which is specifically designed for use in schools in North America, but the syllabus content is in many cases very similar to the science syllabus in UK or Australian schools and could well be adapted to fit in with an individual school's curriculum. One role for school librarians in this area is to search for appropriate websites in the science field and make them available to teachers, with a view to using them or adapting them (with permission) for the school's own use. From the school's own website, material for subjects across the curriculum can be accessed; while most of the material is created by teachers and librarians, some sites show the work done by pupils. This work then forms the basis of new curriculum

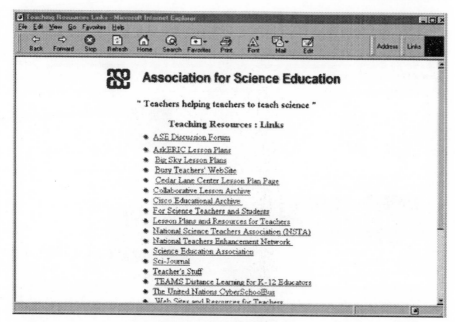

Fig. 5.6 *List of teaching resources on the Association for Science Education website*

material for future pupils in the school. An example of this from Lampeter Strasburg School in the USA[5] in Figure 5.7 demonstrates that pupils can create sophisticated websites: in many cases they have higher order design and web authoring skills than their teachers or school librarian.

Downloading material

Science and other curriculum related sites can also be downloaded from some of the sites on the Busy Teachers' website, as permission is given by the website authors on the website itself. An example of this is material on the National Science Teachers Association site.[6] Figure 5.8 shows material relating to the solar system. Accompanying each webpage on this site is information relating to the content and format of the units and to downloading. Figure 5.9 shows an example of this.

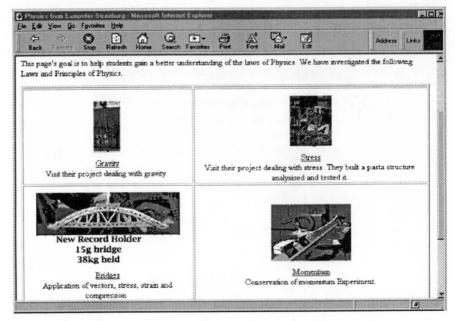

Fig. 5.7 *Physics website created by pupils at Lampeter Strasburg School, USA*

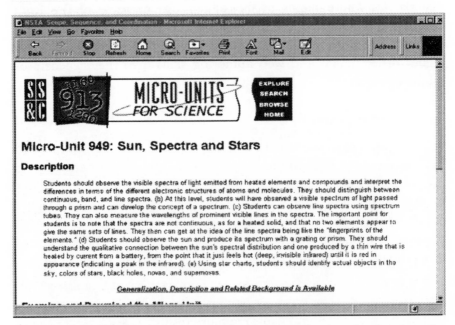

Fig. 5.8 *Teaching unit on the solar system available for downloading from the National Science Teachers Association website*

Examine and Download the Micro-Unit

For each SS&C Micro-Unit there are 2 components: one for teachers, one for students.

The components should be considered as pairs; each pair of Micro-Unit components is available in two formats – an online viewing format and a format suitable for high quality print output. To view a unit online, simply click on the appropriate link; the file will be transferred to your system where you can view it (see 'About' below for viewing notes). To create printed materials, please download the 'print' files as these will produce the highest quality printed materials. The components available for this Micro-Unit are:

Online previewing (complete sets of materials):

view – teacher's component

view – student's component

Download and print (high resolution):

print – teacher's component

print – student's component

About the Micro-Units

The components are downloaded to your computer as Adobe® Acrobat™ files—you will need to obtain the Acrobat file reader for your computer if you do not have one already. There is no charge for the reader.

Fig. 5.9 *Information about downloading material from the National Science Teachers Association website*

Conclusion

In many schools, persuading pupils to choose science as a curricular topic is often difficult once the pupils reach the stage of choosing options and universities report difficulties in recruiting students to science courses. The ASE references at the beginning of this chapter reflect this concern. Science teachers and school librarians have been seeking ways to exploit the information, learning and teaching resources available on the Web. Using the Web in the science curriculum will obviously not, in itself, make science more popular, nor will it guarantee that more pupils will choose science at the upper stages of the school. However, this chapter has shown that using Web resources of different kinds can enable school librarians and teachers to enrich the curriculum by making more resources available for pupils to use, organizing the pupils' activities in a way that makes them more independent learners and introduces variety into the science curriculum. This chapter has briefly touched on some Web resources available but has not covered areas such as online data collection or experiments. The challenge for science teachers is to work with their school librarian to discover more resources on the Web, to explore the possibilities of using instructional websites for teaching and to utilize the knowledge and skills of their own pupils in order to create new and school-specific science resources. The challenge for school librarians is to analyse the information needs of their science colleagues and to seek to satisfy these needs by providing guidance on information skills in science, a range of library based resources and a current awareness service that keeps science teachers up to date with what is available on the Web and how the school can benefit from it.

References

1　Association for Science Education website, ASE, 1998,
   http://www.ase.org.uk
2　Association for Science Education, *Summary of policies*, ASE, 1997.
3　Ripon Grammar School's physics webpage:
   **http://www.rmplc.co.uk/eduweb/sites/ripongs/depts/
   astro/index.html**
4　Busy Teachers' WebSite:
   http://www.ceismc.gatech.edu.busyt.physics.html
5　Lampeter Strasburg School website:
   http://www.iu13.k12pa.us/lampstras.html
6　National Science Teachers Association website:
   http://www.gsh.org/nsta_scripts/mu_record.idc

Chapter 6
Geography

Having read this chapter, you will be able to:

✔ **evaluate the potential of using the Internet within the geography curriculum**

✔ **explore the possibilities of downloading websites related to geography**

✔ **adapt the ideas in the case studies for use in your own school**

✔ **think about ways in which staff in your school can work together to add value to the geography curriculum by using the Internet.**

The National Curriculum

The Geographical Association's Information Technology Working Group's website,[1] which is housed at BECTa's Virtual Teacher Centre, identifies the requirements of the UK National Curriculum in relation to geography and IT capability. These have now been produced in a leaflet entitled *Geography: a pupil's entitlement to IT*. This document states that pupils should be able to use IT in order to:

- enhance their skills of geographical enquiry
- gain access to a wide range of geographical knowledge and information sources
- deepen their understanding of environmental and spatial relationships
- experience alternative images of people, place and environment
- consider the wider impact of IT on people, place and environment.[2]

The leaflet also outlines how schools can implement the guidelines, and includes a checklist for using IT and planning for entitlement for an individual school.

The National Curriculum guidelines also state that 'Pupils should be given opportunities, where appropriate, to develop and apply their IT capability in their study of Geography'. The strands that are most relevant to Geography are:

- communicating information which involves modifying and presenting information in a variety of ways incorporating words, pictures, numbers and sound
- handling information which involves storing, retrieving and presenting factual and fictional information
- measurement and control which involves developing sets of instructions to control events and using a system to respond to data from sensors
- modelling which involves using simulations of real or imaginary events to identify changes and trends.[3]

Within geography, it is expected that pupils will progress to being 'largely autonomous' users of IT and should gain knowledge about the social, economic and political implications of IT for society. It is within this context that this chapter will seek to examine ways in which Web resources can be used to enhance the geography curriculum by examining two case studies of UK schools where the school librarian and geography teachers have worked jointly to integrate Web and other school resources.

Case study: Cowes High School, Isle of Wight, England

Cowes High School is a technology college. It is very well equipped, with a Research Machines PC network of 100 workstations. The library and ICT centre has 20 multimedia computers with access to the Internet and an intranet, e-mail and one station with video-conferencing facilities. The school librarian works closely with colleagues across the curriculum, and CD-ROMs, the Internet and the intranet have become the major resources for coursework and information handling. In year 9 (ages 13–14), pupils at Cowes High School complete a six-week programme relating to volcanoes and earthquakes with particular attention in the first term to the city of Kobe, which was devastated by an earthquake. The pupils' task was to produce a written report on the effects of the Kobe earthquake; this report could be submitted in a number of formats, such as a newspaper report. Figure 6.1 shows the outline syllabus for this programme.

Information resources

The pupils were expected to use the different kinds of resources available in the school library and the classroom. These included geography text-books in the school library, such as *Key geography interactions* and *The wider world*, as well as more specific titles, such as *Earthquakes and volcanoes* and *Natural disasters – volcanoes*. The school library has a range of CD-ROMs, such as Encarta, World Book and Grolier encyclopedias; World Atlas; and newspapers on CD-ROM, including the *Guardian* and the *Times*.

Year 9 Geography Syllabus

A) Tectonic processes
Timing: 6 weeks
Area coverage: local to global (Montserrat, Kobe, San Francisco, Sicily)
Resources: Waugh, D: Key geographical interactions; GCSE texts, various videos – see list; Plates outline jigsaw; Violent Earth CD-ROM, Internet, Reuters

1. The earth's interior
2. Plate boundaries
3. Distribution of earthquakes and volcanoes
4. Plate collision
5. What are volcanoes?
6. What happens in an earthquake

Pupils should undertake one major piece of research homework covering case study examples of either a volcanic eruption or an earthquake (both if possible) emphasizing both the causes and consequences of the natural disaster.

Key words:

Mantle	Crust	Core	Plate boundary
Volcano	Ash	Dust	Volcanic bombs
Crater	Cone	Magma	Vent
Lava	Active	Extinct	Earthquake
Epicentre			

Fig. 6.1 *Year 9 geography syllabus for pupils in Cowes High School, Isle of Wight, England*

In addition to this, the school librarian and the geography teacher did preliminary research on the Web in order to produce a Kobe file of prints-out from a range of websites, and this file was kept in the classroom and the school library.

Using websites

The key Web resources used by the teacher and the school librarian to prepare for this project include general sites such as Research Machines' library site at **http://livlib.eduweb.co.uk/library/** and a general resource site at **http://www.schoolzone.co.uk.** The key sites for pupils include the Kobe sites, which provide details and analysis of the Kobe earthquake. Figure 6.2 shows the homepage of the earthquake site, which contains much information both on the earthquake and its effects on the city. Pupils could select from the list of contents, as seen in Figure 6.3.

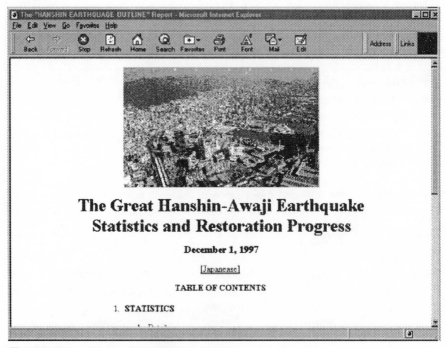

Fig. 6.2 *Kobe City earthquake home page*

STATISTICS
  1. Details
  2. Damage

RESTORATION PROGRESS
  1. Evacuation Shelters, Temporary Housing, Debris Removal
  2. Permanent Housing
  3. Land Readjustment Projects
  4. Socioeconomic Rehabilitation and Welfare Programs
  5. Economic Revitalization
  6. The Port of Kobe
  7. Promoting Safe Urban Development
  8. Public Services
  9. Transportation Network
  10. Special Restoration Projects
  11. Other Measures

Fig. 6.3 *Range of information on the Kobe City earthquake used by pupils in Cowes High School, Isle of Wight, England*

Information skills

In order to gain maximum benefit from using websites such as this, pupils were reminded of the need for them to put into practice the same range of information skills as they would using one of the printed resources. Thus, given the choice of options in Figure 6.3 or in Figure 6.4 (from another Kobe website), it is important that individual pupils or groups of pupils plan their work in advance so that they can select the material that is relevant to their own purpose.

Using graphics

Pupils must also be aware of the possibilities of using the range of graphical material available in sites, such as that shown in Figure 6.5. Pupils were taught to select graphics as they select information, i.e. in relation to their purpose and to select only those graphics that are directly relevant to the focus of their particular report – pupils cannot cover *all* aspects of the Kobe earthquake in one report. Both the school librarian and the teacher acted as supervisors and facilitators for pupils in their use of the resources, and much work was done in the classroom in planning the content and format of the individual pupil's report. By using thinking skills, concept maps, key-word maps and discussing their ideas with the teacher, the pupils can be

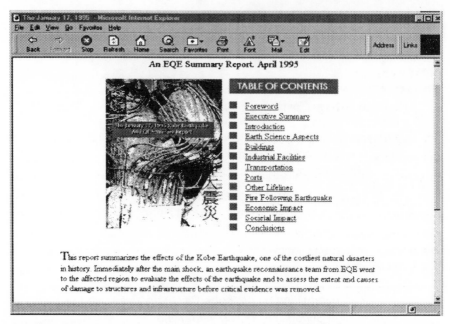

Fig. 6.4 *Further information on the Kobe City earthquake*

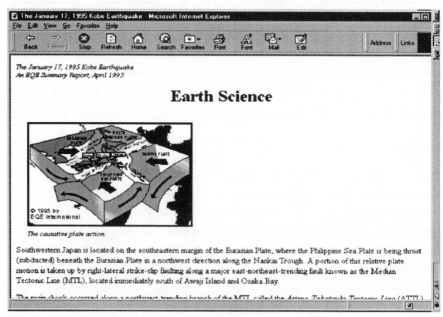

Fig. 6.5 *Example of graphical material on Kobe City earthquake used by pupils in Cowes High School, Isle of Wight, England*

well prepared for using the various information resources available. Because the websites are very detailed, it was stressed to pupils that if they do not plan well ahead, they may have problems in dealing with the content of the websites.

Evaluation of the programme

The key objectives of the geography teacher and the school librarian were to provide pupils with an extra dimension to the information resources used to cover this part of the syllabus, and it was found that pupils responded very well and became very interested in their individual projects. When pupils are provided with an extended range of information resources – they were given direction to some websites but could also follow up links from these sites – it is important that they are taught how to restrict their searching, to skim and scan websites and judge websites on aspects such as level of language and use of difficult terminology. The teacher and the school librarian felt that pupils learned much from doing the project work, as the pupils learned more not only about earthquakes and Kobe but also about the process of planning, searching, note-taking and writing. One negative aspect of this kind of teaching is that it inevitably adds extra work to the role of both the school librarian and the teacher, as they both did extensive and time-consuming searches on the Web to find websites suitable for the topic and the level of the pupils. Finding sites that were useable by all pupils but also challenging for the more able pupils proved difficult.

Case study: Linlithgow Academy, West Lothian, Scotland

Linlithgow Academy is a state secondary school that has been a pioneer in the UK in developing the use of the Internet in schools and in developing a school intranet (see Chapter 11). The school has a progressive IT committee which has developed the use of IT across the curriculum and attracted external funding from local companies and much help from parents that work in the computer industry. With regard to IT the school's philosophy is that IT is a tool for learning and a support to the curricular and social development of the pupils, as well as being an aid to staff development. The IT committee includes members of senior management, subject teachers and the school librarian. Much work has been done by the school librarian in exploring the possibilities of downloading websites for use offline by pupils and permission to use several sites has been obtained. The issue of copyright is still problematic with many websites, however. The geography department in the school have been keen users of IT for some time and were keen to exploit the Internet as a curricular resource. With the help of the school librarian, a number of projects have been developed at various levels of the school, relating to areas of the geography syllabus on topics such as rainforests, earthquakes and volcanoes, urban development and, the focus of this case study, hurricanes and tornadoes.

Hurricanes and tornadoes

The pupils doing this topic in geography were in S1 (year 1 of secondary school). They had experience of using a range of information sources via the school's cross-curricular information skills programme and had used books, journals, CD-ROMs and the Internet before completing this piece of coursework. The task set for the pupils is shown in Figure 6.6. The pupils were advised that their assignments will be marked in relation to: collecting and recording information, analysing information and presentation. They were reminded by the teacher and the school librarian in the written outline of the assignment that they should not copy material from books or the Internet, that they should ask themselves whether they understand what they have read and that when they use electronic sources they should 'not merely hand in printouts, but try to process this information e.g. cut out some sections and include data from another source'.

Hurricanes and tornadoes
In this section, you will use a variety of information sources . . . *books, magazines, Internet material* and *videos* to produce an *investigation* on **Hurricanes** and **Tornadoes** . . . you can also use material of your own if you want.

Instructions
1. Include descriptions of what these features are, why and where they occur in North and Central America.
2. [Describe the] effects of these natural disasters.
3. [Describe what] can be done to reduce these effects.
4. Use maps, diagrams, figures etc . . . colour will help to improve the appearance of your account.

Fig. 6.6 *Geography assignment for pupils in Linlithgow Academy, West Lothian, Scotland*

Information sources

The pupils were guided in what they should use in the school library with lists of resources prepared by the school librarian and the teacher. For this topic, pupils were advised that they could consult reference books such as *World book encyclopedia of science: planet earth*; CD-ROMs such as *National geographic* or *World's weather*; journals such as the *National geographic*; daily newspapers such as the *Scotsman* or *Daily Telegraph*; books such as *Hurricanes and typhoons* by J. Dineen or *Weather and climate* by K. Lye; and websites such as the *USA today* site. As was seen above, pupils were expected to combine knowledge from a range of sources as part of their assignment; in this school pupils are accustomed to using Web sources even in year 1, so they quickly get over any novelty value attached to using the Internet.

Using the websites

The teacher and the school librarian organized the class in such a way that half the class worked in the classroom and the other half worked in the library on alternate days during this part of the geography syllabus. This helped to lessen the load on both the Internet access and the staff. The pupils accessed the *USA today* site after discussing the value of using such a site, i.e. it belongs to a recognized US company, and therefore the information contained in the site should be valid. Figure 6.7 shows the hurricane page on the site. As can be seen, this page presents the pupils with a large number of options to follow up links, and, as with the Cowes High School example above, pupils were taught the importance of planning their assignments before they undertook searches for information and selecting keywords in relation to the aspect of hurricanes and tornadoes that they wished to cover. Selecting and rejecting information were seen as key skills, and there was an emphasis on understanding the text within the website. The *USA today* page in Figure 6.7 offers pupils access to the FAQ (frequently asked questions) service under the heading of 'Ask Jack'; they can learn that this is often a short cut to gaining basic information.

By selecting 'The basics' option on the webpage in Figure 6.7, pupils were taken to subsequent pages that provided them with information about all elements of the causes, development and effects of hurricanes. By choosing a graphics option, pupils could access further information, such as that shown in Figure 6.8. Again, selection and rejection skills were vital

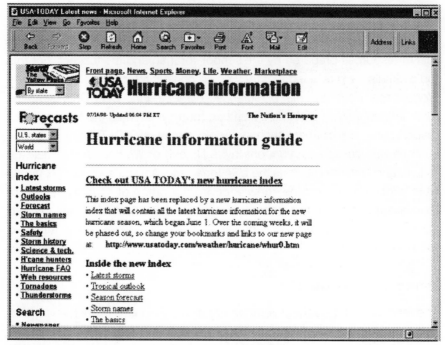

Fig. 6.7 *Hurricane page from US Today website*

as this page also presented pupils with a large number of options. The school librarian and the teacher found that it was necessary to remind pupils that they only had a limited amount of time to search for information and that they should resist following up links that were not relevant to their own purpose. One of the problems in using the Web in this way is that pupils become engrossed in the topic and want to find out much more than the basic outline of the topic. The geography teacher and the school librarian stated that this was a good learning experience for pupils as the curriculum demanded that topics be covered in a limited period and pupils had to be selective in what they read.

Evaluation of the assignment

The integration of a range of sources on hurricanes and tornadoes proved to be something that motivated the pupils to learn in more depth than they might otherwise have done. They also learned about the limitations of time and the need to cover specific areas of the topic. Inevitably, some pupils became overwhelmed by the sheer amount of information present in the

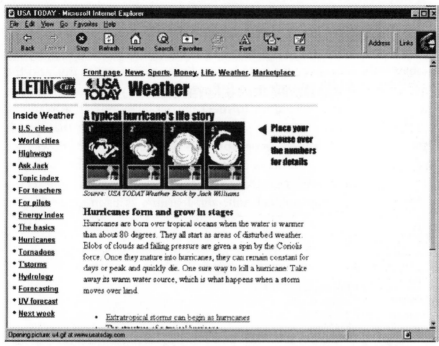

Fig. 6.8 *Further information on hurricanes requires pupils in Linlithgow Academy, West Lothian, Scotland to select relevant information*

webpages and were confused by the amount of detail available. The teacher and the school librarian acted as coaches for the pupils in their searching, reading and listening, and it was clear that many of the pupils who found too much information could learn from this experience and would be able to plan more carefully and be more selective in future assignments. The value of preparation by the teacher and the school librarian in identifying relevant sites and allowing pupils to use some of the sites offline cannot be underestimated. While this inevitably adds to the work needed to prepare for such an assignment, there is no doubt that the pupils benefited greatly from this.

Conclusion

In a recent, as yet unpublished, survey of Internet use in UK and South African school libraries by this author, it was evident that pupils doing geography assignments were among those to make most use of the Web. There is a vast amount of information and ideas on the Web that can be used by geography teachers and school librarians, and there are a large number of excellent examples of instructional websites related to geography that can be accessed through websites such as BECTa or AskEric.[4] The opportunities for school librarians and geography teachers to share information and experience are many, and the school geography curriculum can be enhanced by the integration of the Web and other resources to meet curricular needs. The National Curriculum guidance on IT and geography points out that pupils should be able to enhance geographical skills, deepen their knowledge, and experience environments different from their own. The examples in this chapter demonstrate that using the Web can contribute to the development of geographical skills and learning skills in general.

References

1   Geographical Association website:
    http://vtc.ngfl.gov.uk
2   ibid.
3   ibid.
4   **http://www.becta.org.uk; http://www.ericir.syr.edu**

Chapter 7
History

Having read this chapter, you will be able to:

✔ **evaluate the use of the Web for learning and teaching in history**
✔ **evaluate the use of instructional websites in history**
✔ **explore the possibility of linking history with other subjects through using the Web**
✔ **think about how you might work with colleagues in your school to enhance the history curriculum through the integration of information resources.**

Using IT in history teaching and learning

The booklet *History using IT: a pupil's entitlement* by the UK National Council for Educational Technology states that, in relation to studying change over time,

> In history, teachers need to help pupils to:
> * Identify connections, trends and patterns of change
> * Offer explanations for change
> * Use background knowledge to place specific change in a wider historical context.[1]

The booklet also states that, in history, pupils should be able to establish the cause of historical events such as the peasants' revolt; to ask historical questions, e.g. in relation to hypotheses about working conditions in the nineteenth century; and to write extended essays on topics, e.g. 'Was money the reason why Charles I argued with Parliament?' Pupils also need to be able to handle sources: teachers should enable pupils to:

- Identify relevant sources for a particular enquiry
- Extract sources of information from different kinds of sources
- Summarise the information and arguments contained in the sources
- Evaluate sources and reach conclusions based on the available evidence.[2]

IT sources

There is a range of IT sources that pupils can use in history, ranging from school-based databases, local census material, national censuses, and CD-ROMs to online sources such as Reuters and the Internet. School librarians and teachers in the UK can find information on using IT in the history curriculum via a range of sources, including HABET (the Historical Association Body for Educational Technology), which seeks to support the teaching and learning of history through the application of IT. HABET has a 'Computer update' section in the journal *Teaching history*. This chapter will examine ways in which the Internet can be exploited as a source of learning for pupils by examining the use of instructional websites in history in the case study, and reviewing some examples of how schools have made use of websites to support the history curriculum.

Case study: Hinchingbrooke School, Cambridgeshire, England

Hinchingbrooke School is a state secondary school and was the first school in the UK to have its own homepage. It has been one of the leading schools in using the Web for curricular purposes and in developing instructional websites for use by pupils. The school's best use of such a website can be seen in the World War I website on battlefields. The webpages contain an array of concepts, ideas, hypotheses and information about the war and form the basis of teaching this topic in the history curriculum. Pupils studying this topic access the battlefields homepage (see Figure 7.1) via the school's homepages:[3] graphics and text are used to good effect to allow pupils to read the introduction to the topic and then go on a four-day itinerary of the battlefields. Pupils then have the opportunity to visit the different battlefields of World War I such as Ypres and Passchendaele, and can also access topics such as 'Cemetery details', 'The fallen', 'Personal views' and 'Trench life'. This allows pupils to explore a range of issues including the

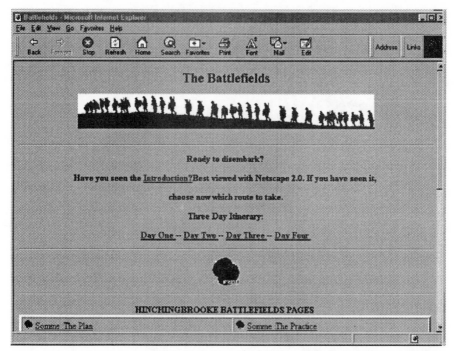

Fig. 7.1 *World War I battlefields web page from the website of Hinching-*
-brooke School, Cambridgeshire, England

military perspective, the environment of the trenches and   the social
aspects of being a soldier.

By choosing the 'Somme: The Plan' option, pupils are taken to the page
shown in Figure 7.2, which discusses the plans of both the Allies and the
Germans in relation to the battle. When doing their World War I assignments, pupils are expected to use the instructional website as an additional
source of information and to select the topics that they have chosen to
cover: therefore, as with the geography assignments in the previous chapter, selection of information is crucial, as is the ability to skim through the
list of options and scan the webpages for relevant ideas or information.

Further reading and links

The website provides pupils with a range of information about World War I
that they can use for their assignment. This is linked to a section on further
reading, which lists books held in the school library:

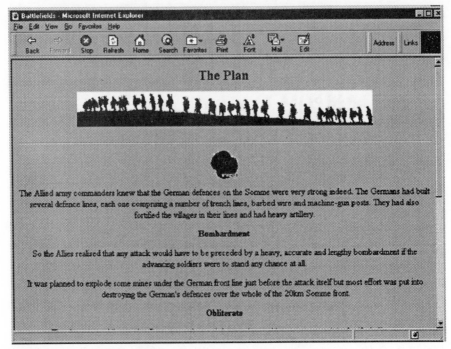

Fig. 7.2 *Allied army plan for the battle of the Somme from the website of Hinchingbrooke School, Cambridgeshire, England*

The Pictorial History of World War I ~ G D Sheffield
Battle of The Somme ~ Christopher Martin
The Airman's War 1914–18 ~ Peter H Liddle
World War I: 1914 ~ Philip J Haythornthwaite
An Australian in the First World War ~ Bill Gamage.

The website also provides a series of links to other relevant websites that the pupils can access. An example is the Oxford University Humanities Department's site, shown in Figure 7.3. This site was chosen by the school's head of resources as being suitable for a range of pupils doing assignments on World War I. The interesting point here is that although the website is produced by Oxford University, the level of language and concepts discussed is suitable for school pupils. One of the issues facing history teachers and school librarians in using information resources of any kind in history is the authority of the writer or website producer, and pupils at Hinchingbrooke are taught to evaluate websites for possible bias when dealing with historical events. This site contains a range of information on aspects of World War I that is accessible and readable, as well as suitable

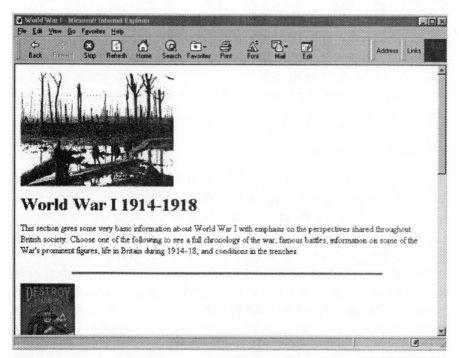

Fig. 7.3 *Oxford University website on World War I used by pupils at Hinchingbrooke School, Cambridgeshire, England*

graphics, and would therefore identify the Oxford site as an authoritative information resource.

Evaluation

Hinchingbrooke's instructional website is an excellent example of an in-school development, created by school staff and pupils, which serves to enrich the history curriculum in a variety of ways. It allows pupils to gain information and perspectives on World War I and to choose elements of this historical event as a focus for study. It also provides opportunities for pupils to use a range of information sources in the school from books to journals to CD-ROMs as well as the weblinks within the site. Although the site is geared mainly towards the study of history, there is a section on World War I poetry that can be used in the English class. The site also covers social studies aspects such as cemeteries and class structure.

There is an emphasis on information skills at Hinchingbrooke that focuses on the pupil's ability to examine her own learning processes as well as merely find relevant information. The use of the website and its links with the other school curricular websites and external links provides pupils with an opportunity to put their information skills into practice to improve their learning and their academic performance. The key factors in the success of this case study, according to school staff, were the willingness of staff to cooperate with one another and to learn from one another's ideas, as well as the technical skills of the website producers.

History websites

There are a great number of websites available for school librarians and history teachers to use, either in the form of lists of weblinks or instructional websites. At BECTa's Virtual Teacher Centre,[4] the Australian WebFronds site,[5] or the AskEric site[6] based in the USA, searching under 'History' and following the topics available will unearth a host of material that can then be judged as suitable or otherwise for a particular school. Some schools have followed Hinchingbrooke's example and produced school-based websites covering a range of features relating to World War I. One such is Highdown School, Berkshire, England, which has created the 'Highdown Hub' as its website.[7] The school views the Hub as 'a model of a Connected Learning Community which aims to connect students, teachers and parents together'. The website presents information and links on all the curricular topics in the school, and the history pages contain a section on World War I. Figure 7.4 shows the webpage and the options presented to pupils. Clicking on the 'Role of Women' icon offers pupils information on various aspects of women's lives during the war and includes, as shown in Figure 7.5, an interview with an author on this topic. This is a good example of presenting pupils with original material obtained by the school that is not available elsewhere. The authority of the interviewee is established and pupils can make good use of the interview in assignment work. Extending the choice of information sources that pupils can use serves to make the topic more interesting and also tests the ability of pupils to cope with a range of different kinds of information presented in a variety of formats.

Conclusion

The opportunities for school librarians and history teachers to make use of the Internet in their schools are varied, as can be seen from the examples above. Many schools are now producing information about their own community's history (Hinchingbrooke is an excellent exam-

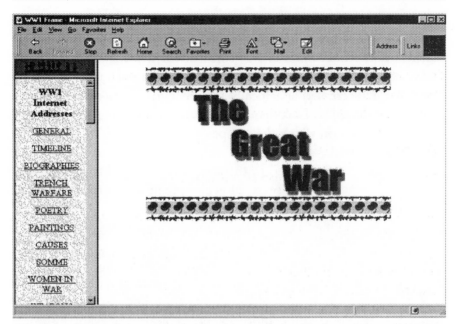

Fig. 7.4 *Information on World War I on the website of Highdown School, Berkshire, England*

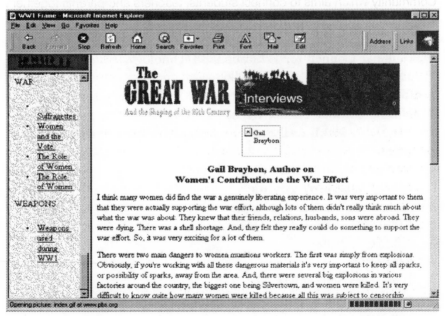

Fig. 7.5 *Interview with a writer on World War I used by pupils at Highdown School, Berkshire, England*

ple of this) and putting this information on their own websites; this is likely to increase in the future. The availability of software that enables teachers and school librarians to construct their own webpages more easily (see Chapter 10) will mean an increase in the types of instructional websites created specifically for the curriculum of a particular school. For example, Linlithgow Academy are planning to develop a site on New Lanark, which their pupils visit each year. The technology thus allows pupils, teachers and school librarians to create new resources that can be added to the school's existing history resources. This can engender a real sense of achievement for all those involved and certainly increase pupil motivation.

The skills identified in the NCET booklet above that pupils should acquire when studying history can be developed by using the Web to good effect both internally and externally. Encouraging pupils to be independent in their search for historical information and asking them to evaluate the historical 'evidence' that they find on the Web will mean that pupils become more expert at asking relevant historical questions and more able interpreters of history and historians. These are valuable learning skills.

References

1   National Council for Educational Technology, *History using IT: a pupil's entitlement*, NCET, 1996.
2   ibid.
3   Hinchingbrooke School website:
    http://edweb.camcnty.gov.uk/hinchingbrooke/index.html
4   Virtual Teacher Centre website:
    http://vtc.ngfl.gov.uk
5   Australian Webfronds website:
    http://webfronds.com.au
6   AskEric website:
    http:// ericir.sur.edu
7   Highdown School website:
    http://www.highdown.berks.sch.uk

Chapter 8
Art

Having read this chapter, you will be able to:

✔ **evaluate the use of the Internet in learning and teaching in the Art curriculum**
✔ **examine the use of online galleries as an Art curricular resource**
✔ **explore ways in which Art websites can be used as links to other curricular areas**
✔ **develop opportunities for pupils in your school to display their own creativity in Art on the Web.**

The National Curriculum and using art information sources

The UK's National Curriculum Attainment Targets for Key Stage 3 (secondary) Art contains the following guidelines:

Attainment Target 1: Investigating and Making
Pupils use technical and expressive skills in recording ideas and feelings. They show a developing ability to analyse and represent chosen features of the natural and made environment. They are increasingly able to research, organise and experiment with relevant resources and materials to develop their ideas. They make effective use of the characteristics of a range of materials, tools and techniques and select from and interpret visual elements. They modify and refine their work to realise their intentions, and plan and make further developments, taking account of their own and others' views.

Attainment Target 2: Knowledge and Understanding
Pupils analyse images and artefacts, using an appropriate art, craft and design vocabulary, and identify how ideas, feelings and meanings are conveyed in different styles and traditions. They compare work across time and place, recognising characteristics that stay the same and those

that change. They critically appraise their own and others' work in the light of what was intended.[1]

From this statement, it can be seen that, in art, pupils are not merely expected to produce artwork of their own but are expected to use a range of resources that provides them with the 'images and artefacts' that they can use to interpret the ideas and meaning in the artwork that they observe. For school librarians and art teachers, this will mean providing pupils with access to a range of art-related resources in the school library and the classroom. The expansion in the availability of educationally relevant CD-ROMs in art was referred to in Chapter 1; along with art books, journals and newspaper reviews, pupils now have a range of sources to use. The appearance of art works on the Web has dramatically increased the range, variety and amount of art available for viewing by pupils. It has also dramatically increased the range of the *quality* of art available, since the websites created by individual artists or vendors of art are not necessarily selected on the basis of known quality in the same way as the art shown in books or CD-ROMs. School librarians and teachers therefore need to select carefully the sites that they recommend to pupils, and they also need to teach their pupils the criteria that the pupils should use to evaluate sites and the art work they contain. This can be as much a part of the pupils' art education as the study of paintings and sculpture as it encourages pupils to be analytical and selective. This chapter will examine a case study of the use of the Web in the art curriculum, the potential use of online galleries and the use of the Web to publish pupils' work.

Case study: St Mary's School, Johannesburg, South Africa

This case study is linked in the St Mary's curriculum to the English example covered in Chapter 4. The pupils are expected to use a range of information resources. The first task they are given is to examine a sculpture in the book *Art in South Africa: the future present* by Sue Williamson; Figure 8.1 shows the pupils' task.

1. Find a picture of Jane Alexander's 'Butcher Boys' in one of the books in the bibliography.

    a) This is a life-size sculpture. In what way does the size of the sculpture affect your reaction to it?

    b) Look at the white figures. List the details of the figures which suggest that they are oppressors.

    c) What is the relevance of the date of the work – 1985–1986 – in South African history?

Fig. 8.1 *Art assignment for pupils at St Mary's School, Johannesburg, South Africa*

Using Web sources

One of the subsequent tasks for these pupils is to complete an assignment that involves using both books and Web sources. The pupils are asked to study aspects of the Polly Street Art Centre, which was opened in 1948. The pupils are asked to write about Cecil Skotnes and his achievements at the centre, in particular his work with oppressed artists. Pupils are guided to the Artslink website and can choose to search using the 'artSearch' icon. A search on Cecil Skotnes resulted in four hits, one of which is shown in Figure 8.2.

Fig. 8.2 *Information on an artist used by pupils at St Mary's School, Johannesburg, South Africa*

Evaluation

The project is organized by the school librarian/media teacher and the art teachers, and seeks to teach pupils about using a range of art sources and applying different types of skills, such as interpretation of art, the links with South African history and the analysis of a key figure in 1950s South African art. The theme of protest in the art curriculum is linked to the same theme in English, drama and history, and the pupils can be encouraged to transfer skills across these subjects when they are using different information resources. The use of the Web has added to the range of resources and has made available many resources, especially via art gallery sites, that would otherwise be unavailable to the pupils. The cost of art books is extremely high and, in some cases, the quality of the material found on some of the websites is equal to or better than that found in books. In this school, it is recognized that using the Web provides a number of opportunities to change the traditional methods of teaching art. The teachers and the school librarian have discussed ways of making the pupils more independent learners and placing less emphasis on face-to-face teaching in certain parts of the art curriculum. The use of the Web has therefore extended the types of learning and teaching that can be done, but has not completely replaced the methods used previously.

Online art galleries

One of the most valuable additions to the resources available for school librarians and art teachers is the range of art galleries that now provide some access to their collections. In some cases, the access to the actual collections is limited, while in others, whole collections or exhibitions of work by particular artists are on view. This provides an excellent source of learning and teaching material for schools, many of whose pupils may never have the opportunity to visit some of the most famous galleries in the world.

The Tate

The Tate Gallery website[2] allows pupils to find out information about the gallery's contents and structure and future plans, and gives an insight into the range of collections held by the UK's principal art gallery. Figure 8.3 shows the range of options for visitors to the site. Pupils can also choose to view pictures by particular artists in the Tate;

Figure 8.4 shows the example of the page listing works by William Morris.

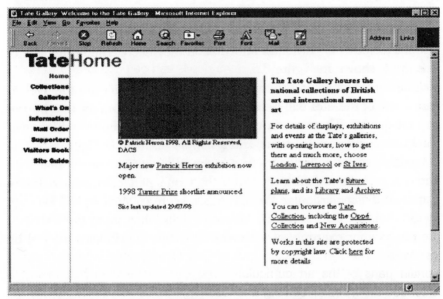

Fig. 8.3 *Range of information available on the Tate Gallery website*

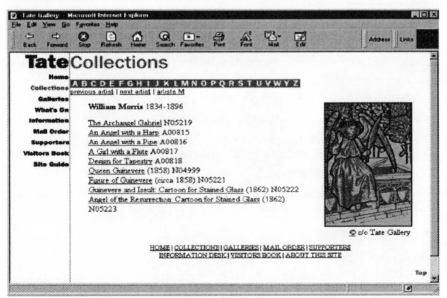

Fig. 8.4 *Example of work by William Morris on the Tate Gallery website*

The Louvre

The Web allows schools access to the art galleries of the world a simple search on 'Louvre' will provide pupils with a range of options in viewing aspects of the famous French gallery. By choosing the 'Welcome to the Grand Louvre' site,[3] pupils can choose from the options to seek the particular information they need. The homepage of this site is shown in Figure 8.5.

One aspect of having the world's art galleries online on the Web is that many of the sites will be in the language of the country that houses the art gallery. There are a number of websites in French that cover the Louvre and its collections, and a sample is shown in Figure 8.6. The availability of art gallery sites in a range of languages means that such websites can be valuable in more than one part of the curriculum. Pupils studying particular French artists, such as Matisse, will be able to use their art skills and their language skills when using the websites. This is another example of the cross curricular possibilities offered by the Web.

Fig. 8.5 *Range of information available on the Louvre home page*

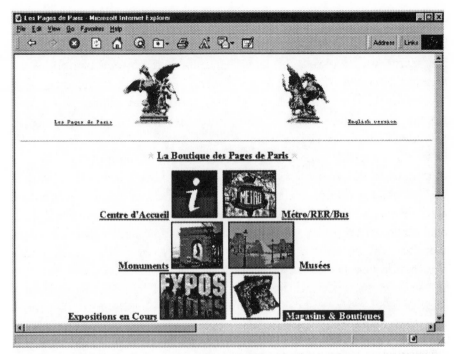

Fig. 8.6 *Example of French language website with information on art galleries*

Publishing pupils' work

The use of school homepages to demonstrate the work done by pupils is now very common in schools. It serves to promote the school and art as a curricular subject in that school. It can also motivate pupils to take more interest in art as a subject. Pupils are very seldom able to demonstrate their curricular work outside the school, but online school art galleries, such as the Cornwallis School Art Gallery below in Figure 8.7, provide pupils with this opportunity.

Conclusion

The National Curriculum guidelines relating to art as a subject in schools outline a number of interrelated skills that pupils need to demonstrate their art coursework. The examples shown in this chapter show how using the Web can enhance pupils' ability to attain the targets set in the National Curriculum, and can allow pupils to link this range of skills when they are researching particular artists or periods of art history or doing research on types of art, such as the protest art seen

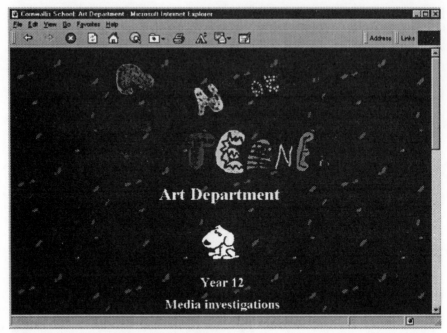

Fig. 8.7 *Art department web page from the site of Cornwallis School, Kent, England*

in the case study. The challenge for school librarians and teachers is to provide pupils with the requisite information skills to allow them to search the Web effectively for art material and to be selective and evaluative in their choice of sites. Art is principally about creativity, and pupils can be creative not only in producing their own works of art, which can shown in the school's gallery, but also in seeking new meanings in paintings or sculptures that they view on websites or in books or CD-ROMs. Art can be seen as a cross-curricular subject with links to many other subjects, and school librarians and teachers can exploit these links to provide better learning experiences for their pupils.

References

1   National Curriculum website:
     http://www.dfee.gov.uk/nc/
2   Tate gallery website:
     http://tate.org.uk
3   Welcome to Le Grand Louvre website:
     http://atlcom.net/~psmith/Louvre

Chapter 9
Other curricular areas

Having read this chapter, you will be able to:

✔ **examine ways in which websites can be used to support the curriculum in a range of subject areas**
✔ **evaluate the use of the Web for individual pupil research**
✔ **examine ways of integrating the use of the Web across the curriculum**
✔ **explore ways of encouraging both teachers and pupils to become independent users of the Internet.**

The previous chapters have shown how the use of the Web, in the form of information or instructional websites, can be used in particular subject areas. It is not possible to devote similar space to *all* curricular topics in a book such as this, and there is no intention on the author's part to try to rank subject areas in relation to how the Web can be used to support the curriculum. This chapter will briefly examine the use of websites in the areas of modern languages, mathematics, social sciences and religious education; it also contains a case study of a school where Web use has been extended across the curriculum and where pupils view the Web as an additional information resource that can help with general study, homework, assignments and revision.

Modern languages

One of the best starting points for Web resources for modern languages teaching is at the BECTa site Lingu@NET at **http://www. becta.org.uk/linguanet/websites/index.html** (see Figure 9.1), which seeks to provide information on its websites for languages' pages in the following categories:

> Organisations for language learning
> The Internet for language teaching

Resources for modern languages
French German Italian Japanese Portuguese Russian Spanish
Other directories of Internet resources for languages
Britain: languages and cultures.

This site gives the school librarian or languages teacher an excellent range of links and opportunities for contacting other language teachers and language teachers' organizations.

A further link from this site takes the reader to the Schools Online Project, part of which is related to modern languages. Figure 9.2 shows pupils, teachers or school librarians the range of options that can be taken up to find out more information or to practise language skills on the Web. This kind of online opportunity adds to the range of learning and teaching methods that can be used to make the modern languages curriculum more topical, to motivate pupils to use their language skills online and to provide links with other schools. Teachers can also find very good examples of sites that cover aspects of language teaching such as vocabulary, grammar and listening comprehension at

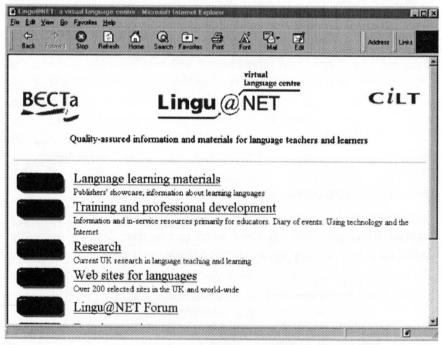

Fig. 9.1 *Options available on the Lingu@net website*

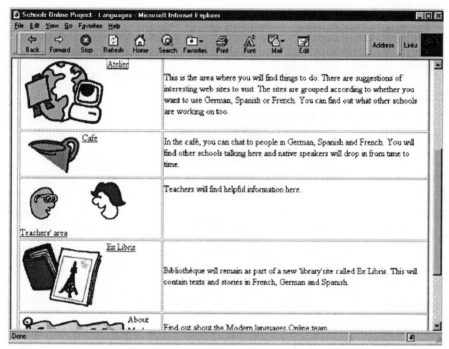

Fig. 9.2 *Information for teachers and pupils on the Schools Online project website*

Lingu@NET's 'Web based activities for foreign languages' option, one highly recommended site is at **http://furman.edu/~pecoy/ lessons.htm**

Mathematics

While there is a wealth of material on teaching mathematics in schools, there can be problems in accessing sites that have direct relevance to the curriculum of a particular school in a particular country, and, as with other topics, school librarians and teachers may have to adapt material that they find to their own needs. For UK schools, the MathsNet site[1] is a very useful starting place, as it provides a range of information, ideas, websites and teaching materials relating to aspects such as Logo, spreadsheets, graphs, puzzles and animations. It also contains articles related to teaching mathematics and an online debate on topics such as 'Is A-level maths getting easier?' Figure 9.3 shows the homepage of the MathsNet site. Users of the site can choose from a

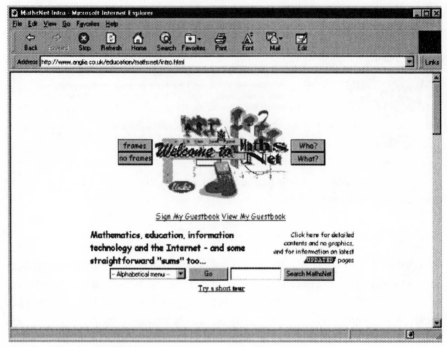

Fig. 9.3 *Information for teachers and school librarians on the MathsNet web-site*

range of subject topics within mathematics, and contains a number of recommended links are given. If the user chooses 'Links on geometry', she is taken to the Geometry Center site,[2] clicking on the 'Educational Material' option, the user can go to 'Technology in the Geometry Classroom', which offers readers access to a range of teaching materials. The site states that:

> These course materials are for a class that introduces pre- and in-service high-school geometry teachers to the use of technology in their classrooms. Participants experience the use of software tools, videos, and WWW-based lessons themselves while studying modern and classical geometry problems. Course projects help them to learn techniques and develop examples that can be incorporated into their own classes. The materials are divided into four self-contained parts: Internet Skills, Classical Geometry, Dynamical Systems, and Symmetries and Patterns.[3]

Choosing the option on symmetries and patterns, the user can access teaching material that examines wallpaper patterns and allows pupils to explore aspects of symmetry by generating patterns via the website. Figure 9.4 shows the wallpaper patterns example.

MathsNet therefore represents a starting point for school librarians and teachers to find materials and activities that their pupils can use. As with the science examples in a previous chapter, teachers have found that their own mathematics curriculum can be enriched by examples from other schools, often in different countries, and that pupils' motivation to study aspects of mathematics can be increased by the use of mathematics-related websites.

Social sciences

Amongst the most useful sites for social sciences is that of the Association for the Teaching of Social Sciences,[4] which aims to provide a range of information, teaching materials and website links for social science teaching, covering areas such as sociology, psychology, politics

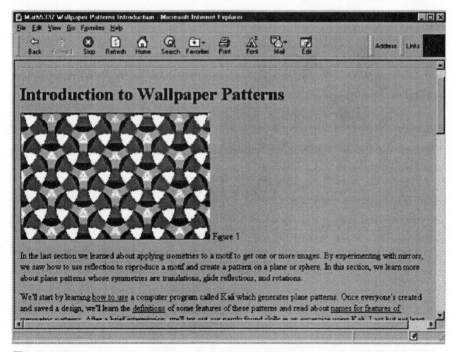

Fig. 9.4 *Example of teaching material for mathematics on the MathsNet website*

and economics. On this site there are many excellent links to topics; if the user chooses sociology as an option, she can go to the 'Sociology Central' site, which covers all aspects of sociology teaching at different levels of education and contains a useful guide to A-level resource materials in sociology. Figure 9.5 shows the main page, which contains a number of options. By clicking on 'A-level Resource Materials', the teacher or school librarian has a choice of a large number of topics in sociology that contain downloadable guides for A-level teaching. Figure 9.6 shows the material that can be downloaded for 'Culture and Identity'.

Other sites of interest to social science teachers include the 'Social Sciences Information Gateway',[5] which is a large site containing a vast number of links to carefully selected Web resources related to social science teaching and research. In the area of politics, one of the most used sites in UK schools is the parliament site,[6] which has a variety of resources designed for use by schools and includes the opportunity to arrange visits to Parliament. Linked with a range of CD-ROMs, books,

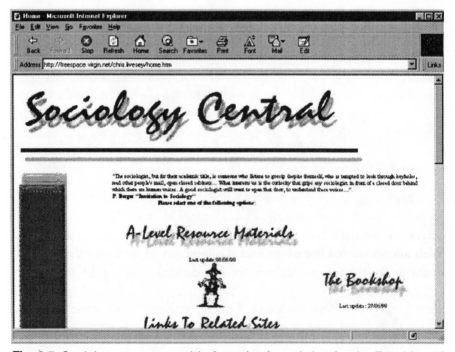

Fig. 9.5 *Sociology resource guide from the Association for the Teaching of Social Sciences website*

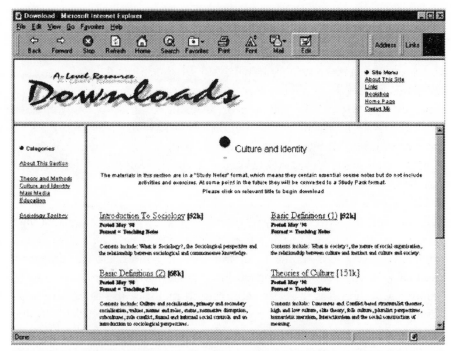

Fig. 9.6 *Downloadable material for A-level teaching in the social sciences*

newspaper articles and journals on social science topics, these Web resources can add to the range of information resources that a school can offer pupils, enhance the teaching of the social sciences and provide pupils with up-to-date sources of information that they can use independently or with guidance from the school librarian or teacher.

Religious education

Developments in religious education in the UK and in other countries in recent years has shown a broadening of the RE curriculum to include the study of a wide range of the world's religions. Using the Web allows school librarians and RE teachers to find sites that are relevant to the school curriculum and are designed for use by pupils carrying out independent investigations into aspects of belief or of individual religions. The Religious Education Resource Centre's site[7] is very good starting point for those seeking ideas for teaching and learning in this subject area. Having accessed the site, shown in Figure 9.7, the user can choose from a range of options. By clicking on 'The

Fig. 9.7 *Religious Education Resource Centre home page*

Lesson Plan Warehouse', the user is offered the opportunity to download lesson plans, worksheets and curricular outlines from a variety of topics within the RE curriculum. The lesson plans and other materials are used in UK schools, and the site is a joint venture involving a large number of RE teachers and school librarians. It allows teachers in different schools to evaluate the materials for use or adaptation for their own school. Figure 9.8 shows some examples of what is on offer.

One of the key problems facing school librarians and teachers seeking useful websites for their pupils is the availability on the Web of a multitude of extreme religious sites, which are not known for their balanced coverage of religious issues. Guiding pupils to particular websites is one way of avoiding pupil access to extreme sites, but for senior pupils, RE teachers and school librarians can provide guidelines on evaluating websites for possible bias and inaccuracy, and therefore educate pupils in the interpretation of material gained from such sites.

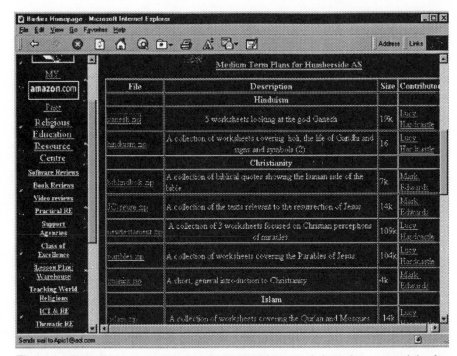

Fig 9.8 *Examples of downloadable teaching and learning materials for religious education*

Using the Web across the curriculum

Case study: Carisbrooke High School, Isle of Wight, England

Carisbrooke High School is a rural secondary comprehensive school with 1200 pupils. The school has been using online information since 1985 and has been involved in a number of research projects related to such information. The school's philosophy is that pupils need access to a wide range of information resources and that they should develop the capability of working collaboratively with other pupils. Carisbrooke High School had access to the Internet since 1994, and the school librarian and teachers have tried many different ways of using it. Pupil use of the Web has been a priority in this school as pupils are seen as an excellent resource for providing ideas, examples and information that can help train teaching staff. The school librarian has learned much from the pupils and the pupils are constantly learning from one another.

The school has tried a variety of strategies over the past years. Initially, lists of websites were gathered from information provided by subject staff, but this in itself was not sufficient. The school librarian and teachers realized that the best method was to teach pupils how to use search engines as well as providing access to good sites, such as ITN and Volcano World, through hotlists. The school also uses encyclopedias such as Hutchinson 1998 because of its British rather than US bias and also its ability to provide access to sites that have been selected and checked. Keeping up to date with new sites is almost an impossible task, and the school staff hope that the National Grid for Learning will provide a good service in relation to the National Curriculum and subject areas.

The school has recently replaced its single computer access to the Internet through an ISDN (integrated services digital network) line with a routed ISDN service via the school's new PC network. The new Internet service provider's subscription comes with a fixed telephone charge. This new service has made it possible to use the Internet on 17 machines in the library and soon on other machines around the school. The school librarian intends to have three machines dedicated to Internet use in the library to provide much increased access to meet the increased demand from pupils at all levels in the school.

E-mail

Pupils at Carisbrooke have had access to e-mail since 1985 and will soon have individual e-mail accounts. Pupils use e-mail to link with friends, siblings at university and other school pupils across the world, and they take part in collaborative projects. Some of the pupils will be sharing their ideas about books that they have read as part of the National Year of Reading project via e-mail. Carisbrooke School has an ongoing link with a school in Denmark and there is regular e-mail contact between pupils and staff in both schools.

The school website

Pupils have managed the school website for over three years. It is the pupils who decide what the website contains and how often it gets updated. As it is the *pupils'* website, it does not necessarily contain information on all aspects of the school. A recent initiative, which has been done in other schools, is to use the website for former pupils to communicate with the school and with one another, and there has been a large response from former pupils.

Teaching and learning

Curricular programmes that involve whole class use of the Web are jointly planned by the school librarian and subject teachers. Pupils can use the Internet for recreational purposes but not during lesson times. The availability of the Web on the school network now provides access from 8 a.m. to 6 p.m.; with the new funding arrangements, there is less worry about escalating telephone bills.

English

Pupils use the Web in English in a variety of ways. The English department is responsible for delivering the communication aspect of the school's information technology programme. In this programme, pupils are required to produce a radio script for a 30-second advert for a new car. They also work together to produce a poster for the car. Until recently, pupils have used brochures for this task and have scanned in pictures, but such pictures date easily. The pupils now use the Web to find the company for whom the advert is designed and can download images and compare their advert with other car adverts on the Web. Those pupils who do extension work can design their own website for their advert or use PowerPoint to present their posters. The Web is also used by the school to promote reading amongst pupils, who can read a range of reviews from sites such as the Amazon bookshop at **http://www.amazon.com**

Geography

The limited access to the Web for pupils has restricted their use in geography, but this will expand greatly with the new network in the school. The geography teachers have encouraged the pupils to use a range of sources, including Reuters Business Briefing, current newspapers and journals, to supplement the Web searches they have done for their A-level work. Other students have done searches related to volcanoes, air quality in different countries and several aspects of tourism. In some cases, pupils can use the same websites, e.g. tourism sites, in different parts of their curricular work.

Science

Staff in the science department have been keen users of the Web for four years. Recently the science teachers and the school librarian jointly organized a whole-day event for one group of pupils who were preparing for a debate on genetics. The group was split and sub-groups were given various aspects of genetics to research on the Web. Pupils learned to use the search engines and, importantly, to refine searches to find specific information related to their own topic. The result was that the pupils came to the debate well prepared with information from a range of sources as they used other information resources in the school library such as CD-ROMs to do their research. Although based in science, this was seen as a project with cross-curricular implications.

Languages

The school librarian and a new language teacher have worked jointly to promote the use of the Web to allow pupils to create tourist information in either French or German. The pupils use AltaVista to search for tourist sites with information on Paris or Berlin, and pupils learn to use French or German as the chosen language in their search. Pupils are able to find tourists sites, e.g. of the Eiffel Tower, in French and produce their own guide to the tower, including pictures, times of opening and admission prices. They also include a map of how to get to the nearest Metro station. This piece of work also has relevance in other subjects such as geography, and it can be assessed for its information technology content as well as the language content within the assessment structure of the National Curriculum.

Business studies

Pupils using the Web for business studies are mainly searching for information about individual companies such as the Body Shop. Pupils use the search engines but quickly realize that many companies can be accessed by the basic format of company URLs, which take the form of **http://www.companyname.com** There has been a large increase in the amount of information on companies on the Web and pupils have benefited greatly from this, especially in relation to their course work for A-level business studies. A recent example was a group of pupils who came to the library to search for German companies using AltaVista and discovered that they could not only find information on these German companies but could also get translations of the German websites via the search engine.

Other resources

One problem that has arisen with the increased use of the Web is the reluctance of some pupils to use information resources other than the Web or CD-ROMs. The school's information skills programme will be altered to take account of this and encourage pupils to view all information sources fairly and to choose the most appropriate source for their needs. In some cases, pupils appear to be able to skim and scan screens of text better than printed pages of text, and this may be related to motivation and attitude to information resources.

The role of the school librarian

In this school, the school librarian is also information and communications coordinator, and is therefore an important figure in developing the use of the Internet across the school curriculum. One of the key areas of discussion with subject teachers is the way in which use of the Web can build on the pupils' existing information skills, particularly in the area of the *selection* of information sources, taking into account their immediate need, the topicality of the information they need and the amount of information needed. This is an issue of debate across the curriculum in the school and many teachers have expressed fears that pupils using the Web are likely to be overwhelmed by the sheer amount of information, lose track of their assignment and be unable to produce good quality work. The re-examination of aspects of the school's information skills programme will include a focus on this issue, and pupils will be given activities in different parts of the curriculum to cope with this difficulty.

Conclusion

This chapter has examined a range of Web sources relevant to the curricular areas of modern languages, mathematics, social sciences and religious education in order to provide a flavour of the materials available and some starting points for the less experienced school librarian or teacher seeking resources in these areas. What can be seen from this review of websites and from the case study is that the use of the Internet within particular areas of the school curriculum is growing rapidly, and also that the use of the Internet *across* the curriculum is growing.

A key issue here for school librarians and teachers to face is how to educate pupils to transfer knowledge and skills from one part of the curriculum to another, e.g. by using the same website for different purposes. Pupils tend to compartmentalize knowledge and skills in the same way as schools compartmentalize subject areas. The use of information skills in using websites goes across curricular boundaries in the areas of definition of purpose, skimming and scanning webpages, interacting with the text and graphics on websites, note-taking and using Web based ideas and information as the basis of a logically structured and well-written or well-presented piece of coursework.

The second key issue is in linking Web resources and other information sources in the school library and the classroom, and, as has been seen in a number of examples in this book, school librarians and teachers often face difficulties in persuading pupils that the Web is *not* always the best source of information available. School librarians and teachers in many schools are seeking to incorporate aspects of the process into pupils' coursework: they require pupils to analyse their use of a range of resources by which they gained their material as part of the coursework submission. In this way, pupils can be encouraged to reflect on their use of resources, and school librarians and teachers will ensure that the full range of the school's resources is used.

References

1   MathsNet website:
    http://www.anglia.co.uk/eduction/mathsnet/intro.html
2   Geometry Center website:
    http://www.geom.umn.edu/
3   ibid.
4   Association for the Teaching of Social Sciences website:
    http://www.le.ac.uk/education/centres/ATSS/atss.html
5   Social Science Information Gateway website:
    http://www.sosig.ac.uk/
6   UK Parliament website: **http://www.parliament.uk/**
7   Religious Education Resource Centre website:
    http://www.ajbird.demon.co.uk/#intro

Chapter 10
Creating an instructional website

by James E. Herring and Adrian M. Hodge

After reading this chapter, you will be able to:

✔ **understand the importance of networked learning in schools**
✔ **identify areas of the school curriculum that would benefit from access to instructional websites**
✔ **evaluate the process involved in creating an instructional website**
✔ **use the Web-based tools available to create an instructional website.**

Networked learning

The development of networks and intranets in today's schools has meant that school managers, teachers and school librarians can consider alternative ways of delivering the school's curriculum. The concept of networked learning implies that a learning experience for a pupil is available via access to the school network from anywhere in the school or outside the school, e.g. in the home, although this may involve the use of passwords. For example, a group of pupils studying a topic in geography such as volcanoes can have a learning experience in different formats and in different places. These pupils may learn in the classroom by listening to the teacher and taking notes, by watching a video, by discussing the topic in groups or by using prepared material such as worksheets in the classroom. The pupils may also learn about volcanoes in the library, where they might follow up the classroom instruction by investigating particular aspects of volcanoes by reading books and journals, using CD-ROMs or online sources such as Reuters, or by using the Internet and accessing sites suggested by the teacher and the school librarian or by doing a search. Networked learning implies that the pupils may be in the classroom or the school library or a school computer room but that they will learn by accessing a website that has been designed in the school to fit in with *that* school's curriculum. The purpose built website on volcanoes can be used by pupils working independently or in groups, and the website will provide pupils with an integrated learning experience that fits in with the rest of the geography curriculum for that particular school year. Thus the pupils may use the website to solve problems that have been highlighted in the classroom but require answers through further research, or they may use the website to learn about a new aspect of volcanoes not previously covered. The instructional website will also include a task for the pupils to do: this may result in the pupils' writing a short report on a particular volcano, which they will hand in to the teacher by a given time. In other cases, the task may be for pupils to do further research and bring information to the next class.

Thus networked learning in schools at present is not designed to completely replace the teacher or the school librarian but to provide pupils with the opportunity for individual learning. Mackenzie argues that the advantages of having a 'wired classroom' are not merely related to the existence of technology by stating that:

> Entirely too much attention has been devoted to the wires and the cabling, to the business of connecting classrooms to the **Internet**. Too many public figures have climbed on this bandwagon as if the mere act of networking would create some miracle... According to many folks, networking offers the same magic as Popeye's spinach .. super powers for an Age of Information.[1]

Mackenzie further argues that his experience with Bellingham School District, which has very sophisticated networks at district and school levels, has shown that improvements in learning have come about not through investment in technology alone 'but because we invested in staff development and we encouraged good teaching'.[2] He poses the question 'What is a technology enhanced, student-centred classroom?', and states that pupils are connected to a wide range of electronic information resources and are encouraged to examine concepts, ideas and information in these resources with the teacher acting as a navigator. The emphasis is on the learning done by the pupils and less on the teaching done by the teacher. The result can be that 'Student questions and questioning become a major focus of classroom activity as teachers demonstrate and then require effective searching, prospecting, gathering and interpretation techniques while students use the tools and the information to explore solutions to contemporary issues'.[3]

Mackenzie states that the use of networked learning, in the form of instructional websites, must be accompanied by a philosophy of learning and teaching that places the individual pupil at the centre of the learning experience. He refers to the work of Means, who outlines the features of what she describes as 'engaged learners'. These are:

- **Responsible for their own learning** – They invest personally in the quest for knowledge and understanding, in part because the questions or issues being investigated are drawn from their own curiosity about the world. Projects are pertinent and questions are essential.
- **Energized by learning** – They feel excited, intrigued and motivated to solve the puzzles, make new answers and reach insight. Their work feels both important and worthwhile.
- **Strategic** – They make thoughtful choices from a toolkit of strategies, considering carefully which approach, which source and which technique may work best to resolve a particular information challenge.
- **Collaborative** – They work with others in a coordinated, planful manner, splitting up the work according to a plan and sharing ideas during the search for understanding.[4]

In short, in considering networked learning, school librarians and teachers should focus on the 'learning' aspects much more than the 'networked' implications of this type of learning. It is obvious that, given the present structure of the curricula in schools in the developed countries, teachers and school librarians will not be able to foresee a complete transformation from learning in the classroom and in the school library to networked learning, but it is important that they consider the possible benefits of *introducing* aspects of networked learning in their schools.

Having briefly examined some features of networked learning, this chapter will now concentrate on the principles and methods of instructional website design for schools, the use of available Web-based tools to create an instructional website and some instructional websites used in schools at the moment.

Instructional website design

A case study

This section will examine the construction of an instructional website by examining the principles and methods used to design a website for a school in Scotland. The site was designed via cooperation between the school librarian and a computer studies teacher who wished to provide his pupils with an introduction to the Internet by means of an instructional website.

Before embarking on the actual construction of the website, there are a number of aspects that the school librarian or teacher will need to consider if the website is to be an effective method of learning for the pupils and not just an electronic form of a classroom worksheet. All Web space must involve a stage of evaluation that firstly addresses the needs of the users of the system. In the setting of a secondary school, the website designer might require the following information:

- ✔ age group of the users (important in relation to the level of language and terminology used)
- ✔ existing knowledge of systems (to what extent will pupils have experience of using websites?)
- ✔ user goals and purposes (what are the pupils being asked to do and what will the outcomes be?)
- ✔ mode of access (where and how will the pupils be able to gain access to the website?)
- ✔ environment of use (will the pupils have a computer each? what facilities, e.g. printing, e-mail, will be available?)

In the construction of the Internet website, the teacher and the school librarian had to consider the existing curriculum and what the pupils were asked to do in terms of individual or group work. One of the aims of the website was to ensure that pupils used a range of resources in the classroom and the school library in extending their knowledge of the Internet as a curricular topic.

The next stage was to construct a paper-based model of what the website would look like. The paper-based model allowed the teacher and the school librarian to examine what the pupils were to learn about the Internet. A tree-like structure was designed on paper, which showed the sequence of what the pupils were asked to read, consider and answer. This structure allowed an analysis of potential problems in how the pupils would navigate through the site. The content of the site was broken down into a series of connecting blocks that incorporated the different elements of the website. Figure 10.1 shows an example of what the first two blocks were to contain.

The analysis of the users and the creation of a paper-based model constitute the first two stages in the six-stage model identified by December and can be classified as the planning and analysis stages. December's remaining stages in instructional website design are:

3. Design: separate information into page sized chunks; connect pages along routes of use and user thinking; provide information, context and navigation cues; create a consistent look and feel.

4. Implementation: create an extendible directory and file structure; use HTML tools where helpful; use templates for supporting consistent look and feel; check implementation in various browsers

5. Promotion: target publicity releases for general Web audiences, potential users and current users; follow online community norms and practices; innovatively connect with users to meet their needs.

6. Innovation: continuously and creatively work for improvement to meet user needs; use testing, evaluation and focus groups to shift and change website's content as user needs change.[5]

Block 1a. What is the Internet?	
i	Introduction: general information; current phenomenon; place in culture
ii	History: where it came from; purpose, people and organizations
iii	Structure/Internet/WWW: framework; technical infrastructure; network basics; birth of browsers and graphical ability
iv	E-mail: history; how it works; uses
v	Hypertext and hypermedia: introduction; concept of links; multimedia v hypermedia
Block 1b.	
•	Exercise 1: How links work; a look at Net basics
•	Exercise 2: E-mail basics
•	Assessment task

Fig. 10.1 *Proposed content for the 'Introduction to the Internet' website*

School librarians and teachers will not necessarily use all of December's guidelines (e.g. for promotion), but this model is a useful guide to the principles of website development and a timely reminder that the creation of a new learning and teaching resource in the school must not only be designed effectively but monitored and changed where necessary. Thus the construction of an instructional website is not a one-off exercise; there has to be a commitment to developing the site in the future.

Navigation within a website is of extreme importance as without proper consideration of how the pupil will be able to move throughout the information space in the website the result may be that the pupil will quickly become lost, disoriented or tired of the system and therefore the topic under consideration. Nielson argues that if a pupil cannot successfully navigate the website, then she may lose confidence in that subject area. Thus, for the designer, a key consideration is how the pupil will move around the website and how she will remain orientated towards a set goal or objective (e.g. the information or the assessment). Poor navigation will be the result of poor design and inadequate linking of the different areas of the website.[6]

In order to help the pupil navigate around the site, it is often helpful to incorporate some form of online map system that will instantly let the pupil know where she is. It is good practice to repeat navigation links at the bottom of each page, which avoids both the possibility of the pupil's getting lost and the need for the pupil to scroll back to the top of the page. For the Internet website under consideration, an imagemap was created to offer navigation and orientation of system structure with key elements of the site, including Home Page, Main Menu, Teaching Blocks 1–4 and Links Page. The navigational imagemap at the top of the pages also serves to identify the site. Above this is a link to the school's own homepage. Figure 10.2 shows the online map system for this website.

The page illustrated in Figure 10.2 shows that the website contains a number of graphical hyperlink 'buttons', which the pupil may click on in order to navigate her way around the site, and helps to orientate the pupil towards the task in hand. The pages also contain a number of text-only hyperlinks, and this facility may be useful in some schools where a text-only browser is used as the pupil may always navigate successfully throughout the site even with this limited browsing facility.

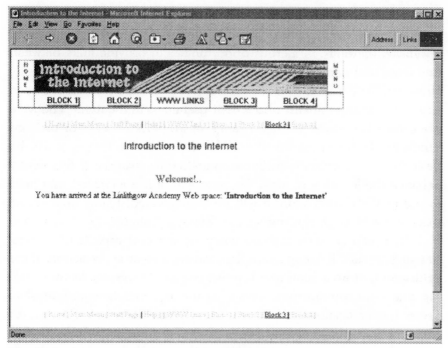

Fig. 10.2 *Outline map system for the website*

Once the pupil accesses the site, she can then travel to the information blocks and on to the exercises and assessment for that part of the course. Guidance through the information structure of the website has been provided by the careful organization of the information into course development areas, for example the division of the course into teaching blocks 1–4, by allowing pupils to travel sequentially or randomly through the system. Thus the website must allow the pupil to read information in the blocks and proceed to the assessment, but also go back to the blocks whenever necessary, e.g. to check on ideas or facts.

The use of multimedia elements in websites on the Web is now commonplace. The availability of sound, graphics and video has enhanced the quality of some websites, though it may serve to obscure the message of others. Graphics should be used appropriately and not merely because they are available to the website designer. For most webpages, basic graphical enhancements in the form of icons are used to represent objects, buttons and other functions. Schwier argues that to be effective, icons should be unambiguous and relatively small. It is vital that the user recognizes what the icon represents and why it is being used. The key use of icons is for navigation around the website. Within a website, there are numerous opportunities to provide links between that page and another page on that site or links to another website. However, the designer must be careful not to use too many icons or to use icons without thinking about their usefulness to the user.[7] The website shown here used a limited range of graphics for ease of use and simplicity. However, as the site is developed in the future, it will be desirable to incorporate additional multimedia material if this would enhance the learning process. For example, it is anticipated that links to actual Web-based sources will be incorporated. Figure 10.3 shows the result of a pupil clicking on the 'Block 1' button.

Thus it can be seen that knowing the *technical* aspects of website design is, in fact, less important than having a clear appreciation of the principles that lie behind good website design in schools. Without taking into consideration issues such as the age and language level of users, the navigational aspects of design and the use of icons, an instructional website in a school may appear to be very sophisticated

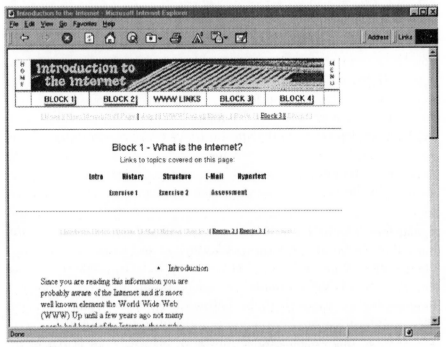

Fig. 10.3 *Block 1 – 'What is the Internet' section of the website*

and glossy but may not be effective as a teaching or learning resource because too little thought has been given to purpose, audience, design, content and evaluation.

Instructional website design tools

The most basic tool for instructional website design is html (hyper text markup language); the most basic elements of HTML can be learned very quickly. McMurdo states that:

> The production and publishing of basic HTML is nevertheless a democratising medium, in that it is fairly simple to work with, does not require programming expertise and can be originated on minimum specification computers. It is an appropriate medium for information professionals, since the importance of the content, organisation and presentation of the information outweighs the technical computing aspects.[8]

HTML works by using a series of tags, which precede the words that will appear on the actual webpage. Thus when the line:

<head>
<title> Example simple HTML document </title>
</head>

is seen on the website, it will appear as the 'header' or headline on the page in the form of:

Example simple HTML document

as the HTML code is translated into a certain font, size and style according to the terms used. Thus <head> will produce a large-sized bold font; <p> (for paragraph) will be translated into a normal-sized regular font. The basics of HTML are very straightforward. McMurdo notes that for more sophisticated webpage development, designers might prefer to use Advanced HTML, Adobe's Portable Document Format or Sun's Java and HotJava but that more advanced programming skills are required.[9] There are many guides to HTML on the Web itself and Hinchingbrooke School's very informative homepage recommends that teachers and school librarians access *A beginner's guide to HTML*.[10]

Software that allows website designers to produce instructional websites for staff and pupils in schools has developed very quickly in recent years, and new packages are available that allow website designers to produce attractive and effective websites without having to learn a computer language such as HTML or Java. The two major commercial packages used by schools at present are Claris Home Page for Macintosh users and Microsoft Front Page for PC users, but many other packages, some in the form of free software (such as that made available by the Internet service provider) or shareware, are available via the Web and can be found by doing a search on website design. The new packages are fairly simple to use and enable teachers and school librarians to produce basic websites quickly. However, it must be remembered that constructing an instructional website is similar to planning a lesson or series of lessons in the classroom or the school library. It *is* possible to plan a lesson very quickly but to plan an *effective* lesson or series of lessons that incorporates the elements of teaching, learning and assessment will take time and expertise. Thus the ability to use a website design package is not the same as the ability to plan, design and implement a programme that will enhance pupil's learning in a particular subject area.

The Claris Home Page website states that:

> Claris Home Page 3.0 is powerful Web authoring software that lets you create and publish Web pages without knowing or understanding HTML. You can simply type in text and integrate images as you would when using a word processor, and Claris Home Page writes the HTML code for you. This intuitive package automates the time-consuming tasks associated with building Web pages. Within Claris Home Page, it's a simple matter to define links and anchors, create tables, and work with frames. The program comes with a generous assortment of 45 attractive templates that you can use as a start for your own Web sites. And Assistants walk you through the process of creating pages and sites, working with frames and connecting with FileMaker Pro 4.0 databases.[11]

This author is aware of a number of school librarians who are working with teachers in designing instructional websites using this package to good effect.

The Microsoft FrontPage website states that the package's

Easy-to-use, leading edge features let you create professional Web sites without programming. Create WYSIWYG [what you see is what you get] frames pages and draw HTML tables in the WYSIWYG FrontPage Editor. Drop in sophisticated, interactive functionality using FrontPage components. Comprehensive management tools let you quickly build and maintain well-organized Web sites. With automatic hyperlink maintenance, you never have to worry about broken links. Plus flexible collaboration features let you work with others on your Web site. Seamless integration with existing content and with desktop applications you already have makes you productive from the start. And strong browser integration makes it easy to customize and view your Web site's content.[12]

For those schools using PCs, Microsoft FrontPage offers an easily understandable package to produce attractive websites.

The above quotes illustrate the basic outlines of what each package does – the packages are very similar. Before purchasing one, teachers and school librarians should try to read reviews in journals such as the UK's *Educational computing and technology*, contact other colleagues who have used the packages, or seek advice from local authority or district advisers. By doing this, they can ensure that the package they buy will suit the needs of their school and will be compatible with hardware and software used within their own school district.

Example

As teachers and school librarians discover the potential effectiveness of networked learning for their pupils and are introduced to the principles and methods of instructional website design, the number of examples of good instructional websites increases daily; it is hoped that professional educators both within a school and across school districts (and the world) will be able to learn from one another in order to improve their instructional website design. The example provided here is not meant to be seen as the work of professional designers with vast experience of using the most sophisticated tools to produce instructional websites, but is chosen to illustrate the work done by school librarians and teachers who have identified potential benefits for their pupils' learning, their own teaching and the extended use of resources in their own school. The example here is available on the Web and should be evaluated in relation to their potential adaptation within an individual school. The use of any parts of this website in another school's web pages would be subject to permission.

Hinchingbrooke School

This school is one of the leading pioneers in the use of the Internet in the curriculum and in the exploitation of the school's homepages for promotional purposes. An example of the school's work is its development of a 'Virtual Fieldtrip to the Battlefields of the Somme'. When the user clicks on this, she is taken to the pages dealing with the battlefields, as shown in Figure 10.4.

Pupils or others using this instructional website can be taken on a four-day tour of the battlefields, which incorporates the major battle sites as well as the main towns in the district, particular places of interest such as churches or cemeteries, a range of people involved in the battle such as a battlefield surgeon and links to other sites connected with the Somme and the First World War. As well as this virtual tour,

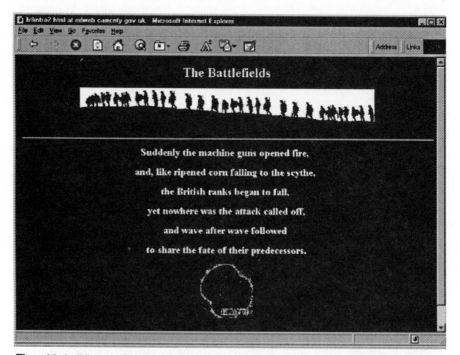

Fig. 10.4 *'Virtual fieldtrip' from the website of Hinchingbrooke School, Cambridgeshire, England*

there are a number of pages dealing with a range of topics, as shown in Figure 10.5.

By clicking on one of the items, for example 'Poetry', pupils are taken to further information about the poetry of the war and then to some of the poems themselves.

The Hinchingbrooke website is a very good example of the use of a range of techniques to make the website attractive, functional and, more importantly, instructional. Authors such as Schneiderman, Cox and Dix,[13] working in the field of human computer interaction (HCI), argue that the key factors in designing websites of this kind are

✔ headings – these should be in different sizes or styles from the main text to help to split up the text for the reader
✔ consistency – this enables the reader to become familiar with the layout of the pages
✔ colours – these can affect the interpretation of important data when used as a highlighting tool. Backgrounds and foregrounds should be

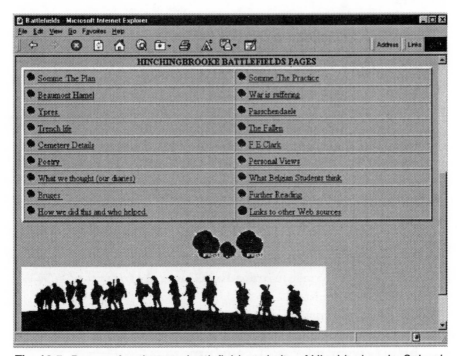

Fig. 10.5 *Range of options on battlefields website of Hinchingbrooke School, Cambridgeshire, England*

complementary and colours should be used consistently. Colours must be appropriate to the use of the site

✔ graphics – these can either enhance or clutter a site; they can be used to add information to the text and can visually show the meaning of an important point

✔ ease of use – the use of icons and links must enable the reader to go back and forth in the site according to need. It is an important consideration if the user is to remain interested in the site.

Applying these criteria to the Hinchingbrooke site shows that the site is easy to use and makes good use of colours and graphics. The reader feels comfortable in the site because of the consistency of the use of icons and links.

References

1 Mackenzie, J., *The wired classroom*, 1998.
   http://www.fromnowon.org/mar98/flotilla.html
2 ibid.
3 ibid.
4 Means, B., *Plugging in*, 1998.
   http://www.nerel.org/sdrs/edtalk/toc.htm
5 December, J., *Web development: processes*, 1997.
   http://www.december.com/web/develop/processes. html
6 Nielson, J., *Top ten mistakes in Web design*, 1996.
   http://www.useit.com/alertbox/9605.html
7 Schwier, R., *Interactive multimedia instruction*, New Jersey, Educational Technology Publications, 1993.
8 McMurdo, G., 'HTML for the lazy', *Journal of information science*, **22** (3), 1996, 198–212.
9 ibid.
10 This can be accessed at:
   http://www.ncsa.uiuc.edu/General/Interest/WWW/ HTMLPrimer.html
11 For more information, see: **http://www.claris.com**
12 For more information, see:
   http://www.microsoft.com/products/

13 Schneiderman, B., *Designing the user interface*, 2nd edn, Wokingham, Addison-Wesley, 1993; Cox, K. and Walker, D., *User-interface design*, 2nd edn, London, Prentice-Hall, 1993; Dix, A. *et al.*, *Human–computer interaction*, London, Prentice-Hall, 1993.

Chapter 11
Developing an intranet

After reading this chapter, you will be able to:

✔ **choose a definition of an intranet that suits your school**
✔ **examine the intranet model presented and discuss its suitability for your school**
✔ **evaluate the experiences of other schools in developing an intranet**
✔ **identify what technical knowledge you need to gain about intranets in schools**
✔ **examine what your own contribution to developing an intranet in your school might be.**

With the rise in the number of computers in each school, many schools across the world have established networks that allow access to software from different parts of the school. For the most part, networking in schools has been of benefit for classes using the school's computer classrooms. These classes have been provided with group access to software for word-processing, spreadsheet, database, desktop publishing and subject specific software, e.g. census software for use by history classes. In some schools, the CD-ROM collection, held in the school library, can be accessed across the network; in other schools, the Web is available at different points in the school via the network. A minority of schools provide access for teachers to pupil records and other administrative information, such as online school timetables. With the introduction of school websites, the idea of making school information available across the school network has developed, and some schools are now considering the introduction of a school intranet that would provide a one-stop access to all the school's resources that are held in an electronic form. An intranet allows the school to provide *internal* access to information resources in a protected environment and the school can decide whether it wants to make this information available to outsiders or not.

Although only a minority of schools have developed intranets as yet, there is no doubt that the combination of the introduction of the Internet into schools and the creation of school homepages, will present an opportunity for all schools to fully exploit their electronic information resources by developing an intranet. This chapter will seek to provide guidance for school managers, teachers and school librarians who aim to develop an intranet that is not merely an administrative device but truly contributes to the teaching and learning in the school through a *combination* of internal and external resources. The chapter will provide a definition of an intranet; briefly explore the technical aspects of developing an intranet in a school; present a model for the content of an intranet; provide examples of schools that are developing an intranet; and discuss aspects such as maintenance, staffing and security, which schools will face in the next few years, via two case studies completed by this author.

Intranet definitions

Mitsubishi define an intranet as: 'A protected internal network using internet technology to provide cheap and effective access to information within a business.'[1] The journal *Intranet communicator* states that an intranet is 'A network, generally operating within an enterprise such as a corporation. Intranets are mostly closed to outside access, but operate with the same features and elements as public-network Internet sites. Intranets are essentially closed, private Internets. Such networks are useful for uniting firms through a common source of information and means of communicating'.[2] An intranet, therefore, can be seen as the school's own internal Internet through which anyone in the school can, if they have authority, access the information they need for learning, teaching, administration or general information.

Clyde cites Gralla's statement that 'When Internet technology is applied and used inside a corporation, and open only to its employees, it is referred to as an intranet', and adds that:

> An intranet is a private network that is created within a company or institution. It is usually linked to the Internet for external communication, for instance by email, and for information searching through the

World Wide Web and commercial online services. However, it is normally separated from the Internet by a 'firewall' or security system, so that people from outside the organisation cannot access the organisation's own information.[3]

Technical aspects

The DfEE in the UK views the development of a school intranet as providing an individual school with access to both internal and external sources of information, as can be seen in Figure 11.1.[4] Thus before a school decides on how it will install a completely new network or how it will develop its existing network, there needs to be an analysis of how the new system (the intranet) will link people and information resources both within the school and outside the school. The development of a school intranet should be learning- and information-led, not technology-led, and some basic systems analysis, which asks elementary questions in relation to the *How? What? Why? When?* of the

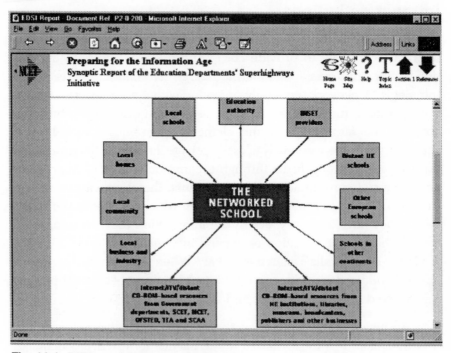

Fig. 11.1 *DfEE model of a school intranet*

design of the intranet, should be done before consideration is given to the technical specification. Using a diagram such as that in Figure 11.1 would help a school to think clearly about the purpose of having an intranet and, having established a clear purpose, the school team responsible for developing the intranet could then face the technical problems to be overcome more easily.

An intranet will be developed from the school's existing computer network: a school does not have to invest in a completely new network in order to introduce an intranet. The school's network is likely to be based on a commercial system, such as Novell; the main difference between a school network and an intranet is that software or information on the school's network may be accessed in different ways, e.g. a menu system, but an intranet will be accessed using a Web browser such as Netscape Navigator or Microsoft Explorer. Figure 11.2 shows an example of the homepage of Highdown School, which is developing an intranet that is accessed via a Web browser.

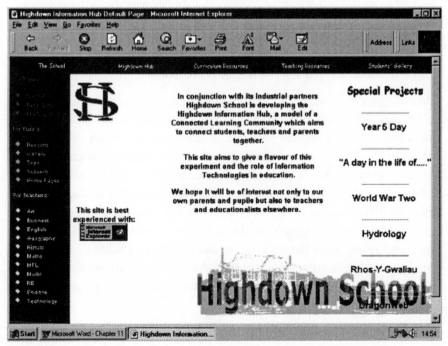

Fig. 11.2 Homepage of the Highdown School, Berkshire, England

Wilkes's survey of schools in Australia with an intranet or which were aiming to introduce an intranet discovered a range of different responses to the question 'Can you provide details of the technical architecture?' Responses included:

Rochester Secondary College
- Main console in CRC/Library with CISCO router to outside via ISDN
- 3 Com linkbuilders with Cat5 UTP to each room
- 4 separate buildings which each have a hub linked back to the main console with fibre optic cable. These run Cat5 UTP to each room in their respective blocks
- Cat5 UTP to each room from Video commander system in CRC
- Each room has outlet with data and video ports, RJ45 connectors
- Student access in rooms to Intranet/Internet with connection to data-port via PC network card for Mac or PC laptops. 5 port hub to allow more than one student access per room.

Mordialloc-Chelsea Secondary College
- Basic setup with Microsoft Select Server Pool (Computelec)
- 2 servers running Windows NT 4 with IIS 3 – one has Exchange 5 and a modem connection to ISP with a static and registered IP address **http://www.mcsc.vic.edu.au** – 203.14.176.154.[5]

One of the challenges facing school librarians and teachers who wish to become involved in the setting up of a school intranet is the need to learn new terminology in relation to intranets. However, while some knowledge of the technical aspects of networking are necessary (e.g. how a server works, how to create documents in HTML that can be accessed on the intranet), the key knowledge relates to the teachers' and the school librarian's vision of what the intranet should look like and what it should be able to do. All schools now have IT coordinators, and many now have IT technicians who can advise on the technical aspects. A number of schools in the UK have tapped the technical expertise of some of their pupils' parents in developing networks and then an intranet.

What information should a school intranet provide?

The development of the *technology* to provide a school intranet should not be the school's main concern in seeking to provide pupils and school staff with access to an intranet. While the intranet will obviously not function without the requisite technology, such as servers, networking software and PCs, the effectiveness of the intranet, in terms of teaching and learning, will depend on:

(a) what information resources can be accessed via the intranet
(b) whether the pupils and staff have the necessary information skills to fully exploit the information resources
(c) the extent to which the school is committed to this form of networked resourcing and learning.

This author has sought to introduce a new term which would encompass the different facets of intranet developments in schools: *school informatics*. This is intended to be a new discipline which reflects the continuing impact of a range of technologies in schools and the growth of intranets in schools in particular. The *application* of school informatics will be seen in schools where the following are in place:

- an intranet has been developed based on the school's server
- school information resources of different kinds are available via one source i.e. the school's intranet home page. The information resources will include
- instructional websites i.e. interactive lessons developed using HTML/Java which teachers and pupils can access from the classroom or school library or computer room or home
- the school library catalogue which covers all materials held in the school library, in teaching departments and elsewhere in the school
- curriculum related websites downloaded within copyright laws
- networked CD-ROMs and commercial electronic online services (e.g. Reuters)
- access to email and the World Wide Web
- school administrative information (restricted access may apply) such as pupil records, school regulations, timetables, past exam papers, newsletters etc.
- some of the teaching in the school is done using instructional websites, either commercial or created within the school or the district,

and includes pupils' use of downloaded websites as well as library and classroom based resources
- there is a coordinated programme of information skills development for pupils and teachers
- inservice training (INSET) is a key priority for the school in relation to the use of the intranet by senior management, teachers, school librarians, other school staff and pupils and the INSET includes computer assisted learning (CAL) theory and practice, the creation of instructional websites and the creative use of electronic information resources
- there is strong support for intranet developments from the school's senior management.[6]

In the business world, Brown argues that companies developing intranets should not see an intranet project as a technology project, and that the key people who should be involved in the early stages of intranet development should be the potential users. Citing the example of the US-based Federal Express, Brown states that at the initial meetings to discuss an intranet, there was no prolonged technical discussions about hardware and software but 'Instead, there were many discussions of 'How should the intranet be structured to help people like us? How can we keep it simple? What should it look like? What should we put in it?'.[7]

Wilkes's survey asked the question 'What type of information is published on your intranet?'. The replies included:

Rochester Secondary College
- Newsletters; timetables; staff-oriented documents; curriculum materials for staff, students, classroom, e.g. revision or test materials, homework sheets, school newspaper
- Anticipate caching Web pages and resource documents through Metamarc Automated Library System.

Traralgon Secondary College
- Interesting links to Internet; Staff phone book (2 campuses); Interactive 'Pink form' for computer faults; Help Desk for Newbies; Schedule of staff inservices; General bulletins etc. to and from staff; Software and CD reviews; New releases in libraries; 'BullNotes' –

teachers' email system for travelling staff; online surveys; Microsoft NetMeeting to permit quick cross-campus meetings.

Methodist Ladies College

- Mimics part of College Internet site
- Curriculum resources – study guides, work requirements, additional resources, online tests etc.
- Staff details – telephone numbers, faculty extensions
- Details of computer network
- Information about College subschools etc.
- Used for communication between staff and notification of technical faults etc. – important in a large school.[8]

Clyde argues that the content of a school intranet can be very wide ranging:

> To quote Preston Gralla again, 'intranets can be used for anything that existing networks are used for – and more.' The school intranet could be used to provide teachers and school administrators with access to the school's databases, including the student information system, the schedule, course information, and other databases maintained by the school. The library catalogue might be made available via the school intranet; already, some of the automated library systems on the market today are providing this option. School documents of all kinds, including curriculum information, might be made available throughout the school via the intranet. Material on the intranet can include documents with hypertext links (as on the World Wide Web); interactive materials; and/or material in multimedia formats.[9]

Deciding on the content of the intranet will require input from all parts of the school, and it is important that school librarians and teachers who have a desire to promote the extended use of electronic information resources in the school should ensure that their voices are heard early in the planning stage. The development of an intranet will require the setting up of a committee or steering group in the school, and it is important, particularly for school librarians, that the steering committee is not restricted to a small group of technically minded staff. The key questions relating to the content of the intranet will be related to the school's own approach to information. For example, some schools intend to allow limited access to all pupil records, including attendance records, exam results and personal profiles, while other schools consider this type of information to be unsuitable for a system that can be accessed by pupils and staff alike, even where access will be restricted through the use of passwords (see below).

The Schools Online intranet project

This UK-based project was designed to examine the implications of implementing an intranet in a school. It aimed:

> To produce a File Based Intranet in each school, tailored to that school's requirements. The intranet would be able to span as many areas as possible including both curriculum and administrative functions as well as allowing for student involvement. Basically, a file based system simulates an Internet like environment on a local server which is used for other purposes. Pages are created on a drive on the server and the Internet browser is loaded onto the server and configured to pick up the set of files and navigate through them in the same way as you would browse the real net. This allows the school to investigate the use of the technology within their own environment with little capital outlay using their existing infrastructure.[10]

The project envisaged a school intranet as both a curricular aid and as a management information system that could be used by staff to access information such as pupil records. Figure 11.3 shows the project's view of the possible uses of an intranet.

Two case studies: Glenwood High School and Linlithgow Academy

In order to gain an insight into the planning being done by schools that are preparing to introduce an intranet, the author interviewed the headteacher, the person responsible for intranet developments and the school librarian in two Scottish schools. Semi-structured interviews were used to gain opinions from the schools relating to their vision of a school intranet, and the issues of content, maintenance, security and staffing were covered.

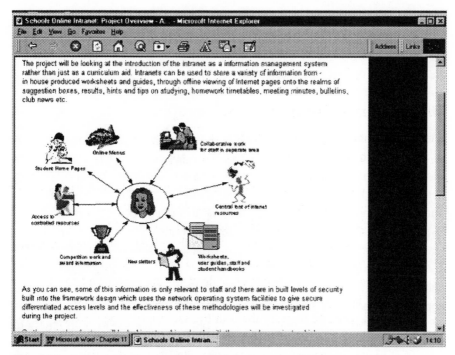

Fig. 11.3 *Schools Online Project model of a school intranet*

Glenwood High School

This is a comprehensive school with 1200 pupils in the new town of Glenrothes in Fife. The school motto is 'Encouraging excellence', and the development of a school intranet is viewed as an integral part of its aim to encourage excellence in all areas of the curriculum. At present, the school has an Internet connection via Campus World, and there is extensive use of the Internet in the curriculum. Campus World is used to support the learning and study skills programme for all pupils in S1 to S3 (years 1–3 in the secondary school), to provide sources of information for business studies and to support the work of the computer studies department, which uses the Internet in all courses from S1 to S6 within the school. In extra-curricular work, the school has an Internet astronomy club that meets at 7.45am, and a modern languages teacher has created e-mail links with schools in Europe and Canada. The school also has an ISDN 2 link to provide video-conferencing links with a local teacher-training institution, and it is hoped that this link can be extended and used for inservice training (INSET) for staff and to develop links with other schools in the UK and abroad. The school has gained funding for a whole-school network, to be installed during 1998, including the upgrading of existing PCs and Macintosh computers and the purchase of the Heritage library system. The system will be supported by a new server and additional multimedia PCs.

The headteacher's view

The headteacher fully supported the development of an intranet in the school and argued that senior management support of such a project was vital within the school. If the intranet was to support teaching and learning across the curriculum, then there had to be leadership from the senior management to encourage all staff to welcome this development and for all staff to be prepared to invest time in the development of the project. The headteacher argued that there was much interest in the school at all levels in ICT developments in education, but this interest had to be supported realistically. It was important that the intranet development was not seen as being imposed either by the senior management or by Internet enthusiasts in the school but viewed as something that could be of benefit to both teachers and pupils in the school.

The headteacher's main concerns related to finance, staffing and management. In terms of finance, the headteacher welcomed the external funding obtained from the telecommunications company BT and stated that the school itself was committed to spending more on IT than it had ever done before. For future developments, the headteacher argued that there would have to be more funding from outside the school and particularly from the local education authority (LEA). The LEA is planning to network all schools in the authority and to provide centralized support in terms of shared learning resources.

The headteacher was also concerned about the staffing implications of intranet developments. The school does not at present have qualified technical staff that might manage the computing side of the intranet, and he argued that it was vital for school management to consider what kind of technical staff they would have to employ in the future to support the day to day management of an intranet. Schools cannot expect teachers to be both educators and technicians, he argued, and if some teachers were to spend time in, for example, sorting out problems with the network in the future, then this would not be a valuable use of their time.

In terms of managing the intranet, the headteacher argued that, while the work done in planning for the intranet development had been done mainly by one of the senior management team, in future there would need to be more input from staff such as the school librarian, especially in terms of providing online access to learning resources in the school. One of the key issues in the exploitation of the intranet as an educational tool by teachers and pupils was the training needed for teachers in the future. The headteacher viewed INSET as crucial in terms of providing teachers with the confidence to use the intranet across the curriculum, and he argued that teachers should be encouraged to view IT developments not as a threat but as part of their continuing professional development.

The assistant rector's view

The assistant rector has been the main driving force behind the intranet development in Glenwood High School, and he produced the specification for the network that was used to gain funding from BT. The assistant rector shared the headteacher's concern about funding and staffing and particularly the issues of technical support and INSET. He argued that all schools would need to review the kinds of technical staff they employed and would have to examine either the retraining of existing staff or the employment of new staff. He pointed out that further education colleges, which in some cases were smaller in size than Glenwood High School, employed IT managers and technicians. Schools with intranets would need to consider making similar appointments, but the question of funding was problematic. However, the assistant rector argued strongly that the school should not end up with a sophisticated network that promised new services and opportunities for teachers and pupils but had used up considerable school funds and was hampered by the lack of technical support. For example, if all staff and pupils were to have individual e-mail addresses, there would need to be technical support in place to manage the e-mail system and cope with user problems.

The assistant rector saw the introduction of an intranet as being helpful in managing school administrative records, but thought that pupil records would not, in the foreseeable future, be available on the main intranet but that data would be held on a different server. Staff wishing to access pupil records would have to log off the main intranet system and log on to another server. He did not see that password protection would provide sufficient security against unauthorized access by pupils. As will be seen below, this is a different view from that taken in the second school in the study.

The assistant rector's view was that the technical aspects of intranets, while important, should be subordinate to the effects on learning and teaching in the school. In relation to the content of the intranet, the assistant rector saw the intranet as opening up the possibilities of greatly increased networking of resources around the school. The new library system would allow internet sites to be downloaded and networked around the school. He recognized that there were copyright issues to be considered but argued that the Internet at present was costly, the content was very variable and the systems were unreliable. Mediation was therefore crucial, and the school librarian should be the key internet mediator in the school.

In relation to the creation of instructional websites, the assistant rector argued that, while this was appealing in theory, a number of factors were likely to militate against in-school creation of websites by teachers. He argued that the time factor was of crucial importance – teachers were under pressure from a variety of sources and it was unlikely that they would be able to find time to produce subject-based instructional websites. However, the assistant rector did foresee the use of electronic worksheets and outlines of courses and available electronic resources, with all these accessible by pupils (and parents) through the intranet.

The assistant rector also made clear that pupils would need the skills to use the information resources available on the intranet effectively and that cross-curricular development of information skills embedded into the subject area's teaching programme was vital. The school was reviewing its existing learning and study skills programme partly to take account of the impact of electronic information resources.

The school librarian's view

The present temporary school librarian has little experience of using electronic information resources and there will be a new appointment of a more experienced school librarian in the future. Despite this, the school librarian saw the installation of an intranet as potentially a very positive development for the library and the school librarian. In her opinion, the library was not being exploited sufficiently in the school, but there had been interest shown by a number of teachers in widening pupil access to information for project work and linking this to the development of a replacement for the present learning and study skills programme.

The school librarian saw great potential in networking CD-ROMs and making available downloaded websites, though she did not at present have the skills to do this. She viewed these developments as a means of raising the profile of the library and extending recognition of the professional expertise of the school librarian. She also thought that the use of electronic sources of information would enhance the use of existing print resources within the library, particularly in relation to pupils' project work. She stated that if such developments were to take place in schools, the school librarian would need to extend her present role, becoming much more involved in cooperating with teachers in the use of electronic information resources and advising teachers on the availability and quality of information to be accessed through Internet sites or via other electronic sources of information.

The school librarian also saw the introduction of the Heritage system as being crucial to the increased use of resources within the school, as this system had many advantages, not least that it could be networked within the school. With the new system, pupils and teachers would be able to gain access not only to the library catalogue (information about information) but also to actual information in the form of full-text sources, particularly from the Internet. One of the new skills that she saw as being necessary for school librarians in the near future was greater technical knowledge in the use of the Internet and how to influence the development of the school's intranet. In her opinion, many school librarians lacked the confidence to take part in discussions about network developments as they lacked the necessary technical knowledge. She argued that, as with teachers, the need for INSET was crucial, and that INSET should be focused not just on the technical skills of intranet use but on the methods that might be used to integrate electronic information resources in all areas of the school curriculum. She hoped that when INSET was available for teachers, the school librarian would be seen as needing the same INSET and would be given the opportunity to join with teachers in training related to curricular developments.

Linlithgow Academy

This is a comprehensive school with 900 pupils in West Lothian. The school has been one of the pioneers in the UK in introducing networking and exploiting the use of electronic information resources such as CD-ROMs and the Internet. The school's headteacher has a very entrepreneurial approach to developing the school's resources to improve teaching and learning, and the school has gained the support of its community in many ways, such as the professional expertise of some parents who have, in effect, acted as IT consultants on a free basis. The school has been provided with funds, hardware, software and expertise by Sun and Hewlett Packard computer companies, and was given a broadband internet link by the cable company Telewest. Since then the local authority has been developing an LEA-wide network to link all West Lothian schools, and the example of Linlithgow Academy has been followed very closely. The school's existing network provides facilities for teachers to access e-mail and school administrative information on desktop computers, and IT is viewed by the staff in this school not as a novelty but as a valuable educational tool.

The headteacher's view

The headteacher's main concerns related to technical support and INSET. He was aware that intranet development in the school would be costly and that funds would have to found within the school and externally. However, as this school has an excellent track record in raising external funds for IT developments, the headteacher was confident that extra money could be raised for hardware and software developments. He did comment that schools are now facing expenditure on a scale previously not seen in the school sector of education, and that schools and LEAs would have to learn how to manage any increase in funding.

The headteacher argued that what was vital in relation to intranet developments in the future was the need for each school to have a clear vision of where it wanted to go in educational terms and where it was possible to exploit IT developments in order to achieve that educational vision. He recognized that developments in IT are so dramatic that having a clear vision is difficult. Thus, looking five years ahead might be problematic, given that five years ago few schools had knowledge of the possible impact that Internet developments might have on education.

The headteacher stated that while finance was being made available for hardware and software development, schools were not being funded to provide technical support for IT innovations such as a school intranet. He said that the school would have to review its present technical support and seek to appoint new technical staff (possibly following retirements) who were IT trained or to retrain existing staff. Compared to the early 1990s, there now appeared to be less demand for audiovisual technician support in the school, and the priority now was to recruit IT technicians. The headteacher saw a further difficulty in that recruiting IT qualified staff would not be easy as schools could not offer competitive salaries compared to industry. He foresaw the need for a school network manager, but admitted that the person recruited would be someone without great experience because of the salary on offer.

The headteacher saw INSET as crucial and he hoped that the funding for IT-related INSET would increase following government initiatives, but he noted that recent funding from the LEA for school networking had not included support for staff INSET. He said that unless teachers were given adequate INSET opportunities to learn about the curricular use of intranet resources (and not merely the technical aspects), the staff would not be able to exploit the new technology effectively. It might be possible to make some use of parental expertise in this area, he added, and also to attract expertise from previous sponsors of the school.

Finally, the headteacher noted that there had been a significant culture change in the school over the past few years and that 'bastions of indifference' had been broken down in many parts of the school. There now existed the willingness of staff to continue the learning process and to make the most of the new opportunities offered by the development of an intranet.

The deputy headteacher's view

In Linlithgow Academy the deputy headteacher chaired the school's ICT Development Group and had the main responsibility for IT developments in the school. He argued that an intranet must provide easy access for staff and pupils and must be capable of providing e-mail and central file space for all staff and students. There also needed to be a cross platform network capable of providing access through either Macintosh computers (which dominate the school sector in Scotland) or PCs. Staff and pupils should view the intranet as being tied into the curriculum and used to provide material and information that can be used in learning and teaching.

In terms of the content of the intranet, the deputy headteacher said that as much school information as possible should be held electronically. Information about courses, including the curriculum, performance indicators, course material, such as worksheets, assignments and tests; and resources, such as books, journal articles, CD-ROMs and websites should all be included, and access to this information should be for staff, pupils and parents from within the school and externally. One key role for the school librarian that the deputy headteacher identified was as a provider of downloaded Internet sites that had been evaluated for curricular use. The school librarian would need to have knowledge of the curriculum, teaching methods, schedules of work and pupil level as well as knowledge of the criteria for selecting websites. Teachers themselves would also be involved in selecting websites, but the time factor might militate against this and the school librarian's role would be crucial.

The deputy headteacher saw the development of instructional websites as being an inevitability, but he argued that there would have to be some pump-priming finance for this to happen. He argued that, in the future, some teachers would develop websites for their own schools and that schools could share instructional websites developed for particular areas of the curriculum. In the long term, this would enable schools to widen the curriculum, in that pupils might be able to take courses, in the form of networked learning, offered at other schools. The deputy headteacher stated that teachers and the school librarian would be expected to acquire new skills in the future that would enable them to participate in the creation of instructional websites, perhaps based on templates designed outside the school.

In relation to administrative information and pupil records, the deputy headteacher did not foresee major problems of security in having pupil information on the intranet. The school already had a network from which teachers could access information such as photograph, name, class, course choice, achievements and special needs, and this complied with the provisions of the UK Data Protection Act. The deputy headteacher said that the school was aware of possible misuse of an intranet by pupils and was not complacent, but he was confident that the level of security and the supervision of pupils using computers in the school would act as a deterrent against abuse of the system.

The deputy headteacher agreed with the headteacher's concerns about technical staffing needs and the need for extensive INSET in the school. Teachers and the school librarian would require training not only in instructional web design, as seen above, but in all areas of computer assisted learning (CAL) if they were to exploit the technology themselves and allow the pupils to gain the maximum benefit from an intranet.

The school librarian's view

The school librarian has wide experience of using a range of electronic information resources and has been instrumental in increasing teacher and pupil awareness of the potential of the internet in the curriculum. He is also a member of the school's ICT Development Group and has considerable knowledge of networking. The school librarian saw the development of an intranet as a logical progression of what had the school had achieved so far. The key advantage of an intranet was viewed as a means to increase the use of learning resources in the school on a networked basis. The library has been a source of downloaded websites for the past two years and many of the sites have been used by pupils in project work. The school librarian saw such sites as a valuable resource but argued that, in some cases, sites could be downloaded, stored on the network, used for a particular purpose and then discarded. New software also allowed the latest version of a site to be downloaded when changes were made to the site. The networking of such websites and CD-ROMs would provide much increased access to resources for pupils and teachers in the classroom, but the school librarian was aware that there might be a danger in the future of teachers and pupils relying so heavily on networked electronic information resources that they might ignore the valuable print resources in the library.

The school librarian agreed with the deputy headteacher's view of the development of instructional websites and argued that this will be a future role for school librarians in cooperation with teachers. In the school at present there were discussions between the school librarian and a history teacher about creating an instructional website related to New Lanark. This website would incorporate evidence of pupil visits to New Lanark, material from previous pupil projects and assignments for pupils to complete by using a range of print and electronic resources. A key factor was the time needed to develop such websites and the school librarian recognized that this could be a limiting factor in the future.

The school librarian argued that INSET for school librarians in the future would need to take account of the new role that they might play in not only providing resources to support the curriculum but also in the design of online materials and information to be used by pupils in the school. School librarians will need expertise in networking, Internet use, information skills development, CAL and networked learning. It was argued that he and his fellow professionals will have to justify their role in the future as key players in the learning process in the school and that it is vital that school librarians are at the heart of IT developments in schools and not on the periphery.[11]

Conclusion

It can be seen from the literature, the examples of schools and the case studies that the development of intranets in schools is an inevitability.

This does not necessarily mean that all schools will develop intranets that improve the learning and teaching environment in the school. If schools view intranets merely as administrative systems that control access to pupil records or provide access to a form of electronic school bulletin board, then the educational value will be limited. Thus there are clear responsibilities for school management, teachers and school librarians to become actively involved in the development of a school intranet to ensure that the new systems provide real value-added services to pupils and to staff. Thus school librarians and teachers should seek to influence policy making in this area by:

✔ working together to discuss the implications of an intranet for learning in the classroom and the school library
✔ gaining an adequate knowledge of the technical aspects of intranets to be able to discuss these with the school's IT coordinator
✔ learning more about networked learning and the potential use of instructional websites
✔ seeking advice on aspects such as copyright in relation to downloaded websites
✔ contacting colleagues in other schools where intranets have been developed
✔ making a case for being included in steering committees set up to decide on the form and content of the school intranet.

Clyde cites D'Ignazio's argument that a school intranet 'offers the opportunity for unlimited student, teacher, and community collaboration without the dangers associated with the larger Internet'[12] and that collaboration between the school's educational professionals will be a key factor in the success of any intranet development in a school.

References

1   Mitsubishi Electric, *Intranet: the business benefits*, Birmingham, Mitsubishi Electric, 1997.
2   *Intranet communicator*, **1** (8), 1997, 31.
3   Clyde, L., 'The school intranet: an opportunity for the school library', *Emergency librarian*, January/February 1998.
4   Department for Education and Employment, *Preparing for the information age*, DfEE, 1997. Website:
    http://vtc.ngfl.gov.uk/reference/edsi

5 Wilkes, J., personal e-mail, 1998.

6 Herring, J. E., 'School informatics: the vision, the learning, the information, the technology and the need for research', paper presented at the 2nd Annual Forum on Research in School Librarianship, 27th IASL Conference, Israel 1998.

7 Brown, E., 'The FedEx intranet style book', *Intranet communicator*, 1 (8), July/August 1997, 4–9.

8 Wilkes, J., op. cit.

9 Clyde, L., op. cit.

10 For more information on the Schools Online project, see: **http://sol2.ultralab.anglia.ac.uk**

11 Herring, J. E., op. cit.

12 Clyde, L., op. cit.

Chapter 12
Future developments

After reading this chapter, you will be able to:

✔ evaluate developments in the future school curriculum
✔ evaluate developments in IT in schools
✔ explore the potential of the Internet in your school
✔ identify areas of staff development needed to keep you up to date with educational and technological change
✔ examine a vision of the future school classroom and school library.

Recent technological developments

Given that, until very recently, most schools in the developed world had no connection to the Internet at all, trying to predict what might happen in tomorrow's schools may appear to be a foolish exercise. School staff are not in control of technological developments but have to respond to them, and it is clear that the rate of technological change is unlikely to slow down in the educational sphere. For example, many school librarians and teachers are concerned about whether their school networks will have enough storage space to cope with a rapid increase in the use of instructional websites in the school curriculum and the use of downloaded multimedia material from the Web. The continuing miniaturization in the computer industry is likely to prove these fears groundless as the capacity of individual PCs or Macintosh computers will rapidly expand, with one PC having the storage capacity of 10, 20 or 100 of today's machines.

Changes in technology will happen and the key factor in coping with such change lies in accepting the fact that change will be a normal facet of work in a school. For example, many school librarians and teachers will be able to remember when their school had no CD-ROMs but today CD-ROMs are an accepted part of the school's information resources: both have learned new skills and passed these on to their pupils. The skills related to using CD-ROMs are initially technologically based (particularly if the CD-ROMs are networked), but the key educational skills relate to choosing CD-ROMs that are relevant to the curriculum and ensuring that pupils have the requisite information skills to cope with the vast amount of information and ideas available. The introduction of the Internet and a school intranet can be seen as part of this continuing process of change in schools, the technological change that requires the acquisition of new terminology by school librarians and teachers and the adaptation of this change to the needs of the curriculum in the school. As will be seen below, technology will not radically change the *content* of the school curriculum but may affect both how it is delivered and the role played by the school librarian and the teacher.

Adapting to changes in technology and in the delivery of the school curriculum can be seen as a potential threat to the professional integrity of both school librarians and teachers. School librarians may fear that the introduction of a school intranet will make their information–provider role redundant as pupils and teachers may choose to use only electronic sources of information to satisfy their needs. Teachers may fear that the development of instructional websites will reduce their role as the key deliverers of the school curriculum and that they may be forced into using externally designed lesson plans with their own pupils. These fears are real, but recognizing that these fears exist and developing strategies to cope with such fears are a first step in adapting to change in schools. School managers have a responsibility to reassure staff and to develop staff in a way that enables them to cope with change, but school librarians and teachers themselves have responsibilities for their own personal and professional development. This chapter will seek to provide some guidelines for coping with future change by examining potential changes in the school curriculum; reviewing IT developments; evaluating Internet developments in schools; and examining the need for continuous staff development in schools if school librarians and teachers are to cope with future changes and harness these changes to the good of the school.

Future curriculum

A review of the literature on future developments in the school curriculum in the UK and in other countries demonstrates that, while there is an emphasis on providing pupils with the necessary skills in using new technologies such as the Internet and an emphasis on examining present teaching methods, there is no evidence that the basic content of the curriculum will radically change. Pupils in the future will still study English, history, geography and other subjects, and will still be expected to demonstrate knowledge, understanding and skills in these areas through various forms of assessment. At a recent UK conference on information technology, communications and the future curriculum, it was interesting to note that all speakers viewed the content of the future curriculum as similar to the present one, though they recognized a need for continual curriculum review. Tate argues that 'the curriculum reflects what we feel about our fundamental ends and purposes as human beings. It reflects those things that are so important to us that we wish to pass them on to the next generation. It reflects the kind of community we would like ourselves to be.'[1] It is further argued that when schools are examining their development of IT, they should firstly ask the question 'what contribution can IT make to our basic purposes and priorities?' before evaluating how IT might affect individual parts of the curriculum.[2]

Many commentators on the future curriculum stress the need to allow pupils to work more independently and to incorporate skills from various parts of the curriculum. Treadaway argues that, in the future, 'the curriculum could be structured into Processes (e.g. Scientific Investigation; Using and Applying Mathematics; Designing and Evaluating); subject specific skills; and content related material (which could be grouped into subject or into different content/topic groups).'[3]

Heppel says that the increased use of IT and particularly the Internet has provided pupils with new capabilities, and that these capabilities need to be examined in relation to teaching and assessment in the future. He states that pupils will develop:

- new competence and confidence in technology
- the ability to engage with and process large amounts of information
- high quality working relationships solely through this medium

- a high degree of critical awareness and the ability to think about the process of thinking.[4]

Heppel argues that the present curriculum stresses the end product too much and that the future curriculum should develop forms of assessment in which pupils are required to review their own learning processes that they used in completing an assessment.[5] Heppel's views correlate closely with the themes identified in this book in that he emphasizes the need for school professionals to examine the learning and teaching in their schools and the extent to which this can be improved by using new technologies.

IT developments

The one certainty about IT hardware in the schools of the future is that the equivalent of today's PC or Macintosh will be smaller, much more powerful and will integrate a range of technologies. In the future, there is unlikely to be a product that is marketed solely as a television or as a computer or a CD player or videocassette player or even a telephone. Miniaturization and integration are the keywords for future IT hardware and software. Radford states that 'micromachines' are being developed where dimensions 'are millimetres at the most. Their moving parts are microscopic: the size of pollen grains', and that these systems will be incorporated into future computers, thus dramatically increasing their capacity and reducing their size. Radford argues that where once having the equivalent of a PC on your wristwatch was seen as science fiction, scientists are currently developing prototypes and that mass production may start in a few years time.[6] The fact that computers will be smaller and more inexpensive in the future implies that schools will be able to afford a wide range of computers for use in the classroom, the school library, the science laboratory and at home. This increase in *quantity* should not be confused with an equivalent increase in *quality* of software or of better teaching and learning in schools, but there is no doubt that increased availability of low cost computers has the potential to be a real asset, in particular to poorer schools.

Developments in software are likely to see an increase in the availability of low cost multimedia packages for schools. For example, the capacity of CD-ROMs in schools is already being seen as limited, in that the ability to incorporate video sequences of any length is restricted. Raouf states that DVD (digital versatile disk) technology may well replace the CD-ROM because of its vastly superior storage capacity: a CD-ROM can hold 650 MB of data whereas 'a double-sided, double-layered DVD disk can hold a staggering 17 GB', which means that the DVD could hold eight hours of high-quality video. Raouf admits that there are few titles available for DVDs as yet, but predicts that CD-ROM vendors will incorporate DVD technology into future systems and that software publishers will seize on this opportunity.[7] There is an obvious educational market for quality DVD-ROMs in the future, but school librarians and teachers will have to evaluate such resources in a similar fashion to the evaluation of today's CD-ROMs and websites, i.e. examine the curricular value of such resources and the information skills needed by pupils to cope with them.

Internet developments

Developments in the Internet will, to a certain extent, depend on the increased capacity of school networks and PCs, as there will definitely be more educational material on the Internet that is in multimedia format. The availability of integrated programmes of learning in curricular subjects such as science or English will definitely increase and schools in different countries will be able to share curricular resources and possibly combine the talents of their best teachers. In a limited way, such resources already exist on some educationally based websites, and schools have the opportunity to learn from the teaching and learning in other schools. The main difference in the future is that while individual lessons are available now, in the future whole programmes of curriculum planning, lesson delivery, resource use and assessment may be accessed by schools. The key issues here relate to the suitability of such programmes for an individual school and include the cultural context of the online programmes, the level of language used, the types of resources identified, the forms of assessment and the format of the programmes. For example, are pupils in a school in Scotland likely to benefit from online 'lessons' accessed on a website from Australia or North America that includes video of a teacher talking to pupils, online resources for pupils to read and view, information skills guidelines and an inbuilt assessment and feedback package? The answer has to be 'possibly', as the school would have to examine what benefits there would be to that school's curriculum and to the learning of those pupils compared to the existing learning and teaching structure of the school. What is not being considered at present is the *replacement* of teachers and school librarians by an online curriculum. There is likely to be a mixture of school-designed programmes available on the school intranet, traditional classroom teaching, individual study in the school library and at home, and access to external programmes. The benefits of this mixture will be seen if pupils become more sophisticated learners and users of a range of resources and gain more independence from teachers and school librarians.

A further aspect of the Internet that has to be considered relates to the increasing commercialization of the Internet and the search for profitable websites by companies. Bennion reports that advertising on the Internet was up 171% between 1997 and 1998, that there was an increase in the number of Internet users of 53% between May 1997 and May 1998 to 92 million users, that commercial dealings on the Internet in the same period rose by 205% to $2.3 billion and that the world's leading companies are now actively trading on the Internet and making a profit.[8] There are a number of implications for schools in the increased commercialization of the Internet. These include:

✔ what is freely available on the Web at present may have to be paid for in the future (e.g. complex searching)
✔ there may be pressure on some schools to charge others for having access to instructional websites designed in these schools
✔ there will be much more advertising on websites accessed by pupils and teachers
✔ the development of very sophisticated educational websites that include interactive multimedia programmes for schools will be accompanied by cost-restricted access.

On a more positive note, the growth of mergers amongst telecommunications companies, such as BT and AT&T, and the increased competition amongst existing Web companies, such as Yahoo!, Netscape and Microsoft, may provide a better range of products that can be used by school staff and pupils in the future.

Keeping up to date

The constant changes in the school curriculum, in IT hardware and software and in the Internet can all seem overwhelming to school librarians or teachers trying to cope with the existing pressures of providing quality education to pupils in their school. In the UK each local authority or district will have its own programme of INSET and each school will also have an INSET programme. If schools are serious about changing the way pupils learn, the teaching methods used in the school and the use of print and electronic resources, then Web developments need to be given priority in terms of time allocated in the INSET programme. The exploitation of a school intranet, for example, can only be successful if there is adequate discussion of educational implications and relevant training. Too often INSET devoted to the increased use of the Web in the curriculum takes the form of a group of teachers sitting at terminals in a school computer room and carrying out instructions from the school IT coordinator and/or the school librarian i.e. the INSET is *technology driven*. INSET of this kind would be much more profitable if sitting at a computer was the end point of an INSET day, half of which had been devoted to discussion of learning and teaching strategies needed to incorporate the Web into the school curriculum. Pressure by school librarians and teachers on senior management who design the INSET programme can ensure that Web-related INSET is *curriculum driven* in the same way that INSET on reading or numeracy would be.

As well as formal INSET, school librarians and teachers need to keep up to date through contact with their own professional organization, such as the UK's School Libraries Group or the Association for Science Education. Such organizations will act as a personal and group information service for new developments through journals, meetings and websites. Most national quality newspapers now have both educational supplements and sections related to Internet and IT developments. In the UK, for example, both *Guardian education* and *Online guardian* provide information on the latest Web related issues in education in a short and readable form. Specific IT-related journals, such as the UK's *Educational computing and technology*, concentrate on reviewing hardware and software as well as providing articles that examine IT developments in particular schools or districts. Subject-related journals, such as the UK's *Teaching geography* or *Physics education*, now often contain information about websites or the use of the Web in these subjects. Thus keeping up to date requires a regular scan of professional and related journals and, where possible, membership of a relevant listserv. Each school librarian or teacher can profit from having a personal development plan to ensure that she keeps abreast of Web-related developments and feels confident to contribute to discussions on how her school can best benefit from exploiting the potential of the Web.

The classroom and school library of the future

It could be argued that any discussion of future classrooms or school libraries is redundant as both will disappear at some point, to be replaced by education mainly from the home, with pupils attending educational centres for perhaps one or two days per week for social education. Whether this is likely to happen or will be seen as desirable in the next 50 years is debatable, but in the near future there certainly will be changes in the school classroom and school library. One of the key changes is likely to lie in the increasing similarity of both places, as classrooms become more like libraries and libraries more like classrooms. There will certainly be more computer terminals and more access to electronic resources, such as the Web, networked CD- or DVD-ROMs or online services, in both. There will be more use of the school library as a classroom because of the access to both print and electronic resources in one place, and teachers are likely to spend more time with their pupils in the school library. Both school librarians and teachers will spend less time delivering planned lessons that last for a statutory period of perhaps 40 minutes. The role of the school librarian and the teacher will be more of a facilitator in guiding pupils in how to use instructional websites or learn from a range of resources. Both will constantly be involved in coaching pupils to use the necessary information skills to identify purpose; seek out ideas, explanations or information for a particular topic; read, view or listen for information; and complete assessments that may be a mixture of written, graphical and oral presentations.

The future role of the school librarian and the teacher should be seen as an enlightening one, with technology being used to improve learning and teaching and to remove some of the drudgery of working in a school classroom or library. By effectively using the Web and the educational resources available, school librarians and teachers can develop the curriculum in such a way as to improve the satisfaction that they gain from teaching pupils to learn and from learning themselves. By working together and allowing their professional skills to converge (just as the technologies have converged), they can provide leadership in the school curriculum. They can work with senior management to develop schools in which all pupils are given the opportunity to be effective learners and to develop into people who will contribute to their individual communities and societies in a positive manner through employment, social and leisure activities.

References

1   Tate, N., 'Introduction and welcome', in School Curriculum and Assessment Authority, *Information technology, communications and the future curriculum: international conference report*, London, SCAA, 1997.
2   ibid.
3   Treadaway, M., 'Information capability 2000? A peek into the future', *School library 2000*, 10, March 1996, 1, 20.
4   Heppel, S., 'Issues for a future curriculum', in School Curriculum and Assessment Authority, op. cit,
5   ibid.
6   Radford, T., 'No small potatoes', *Online guardian*, 23 July 1998, 9–10.
7   Raouf, F., 'Is this the end of the CD?', *Viglen magazine*, (13), Winter 1997/8, 8.
8   Bennion, J., 'The Wall St Dash', *Online guardian*, 23 July 1998, 2–3.

Bibliography

Alexander, J. and Tate, M., The Web as a research tool: evaluation techniques, 1998, Website:
http://www.science.widener.edu/~withers/evalout

Association for Science Education, *Summary of policies*, Hatfield, Herts, ASE, 1997.

Bennion, J., 'The Wall St Dash', *Online guardian*, 23 July 1998, 2–3.

Brown, E., 'The FedEx intranet style book', *Intranet communicator*, **1** (8), 1997, 4–9.

Clyde, L., *School libraries and the electronic community*, Lanham, MD, Scarecrow, 1997.

Clyde, L., 'The school intranet: an opportunity for the school library', *Emergency librarian*, January/February 1998.

Corbett, A., 'How can you integrate IT across the curriculum?', *Computers don't bite*, January 1998.

Crawford, R., *Managing information technology in secondary schools*, London, Routledge. 1997.

Cunningham, M. et al.: *Schools in cyberspace*, Sevenoaks, Hodder and Stoughton, 1997.

December, J., Web development: processes, 1997. Website:
http://www.december.com/web/develop/processes.html

Department for Education and Employment, *Connecting the learning society: national grid for learning*, London, DfEE. 1997.

Department for Education and Employment, *Preparing for the information age*, London, DfEE, 1997. Website:
http://www.open.gov.uk/dfee/dfeehome.htm

Department for Education and Employment, *The National Curriculum for English*. Website:
http://www.dfee.gov.uk/nc/engindex.html

Donnelly, J., *IT and schools*, London, Croner, 1996.

Eisenberg, M. and Berkovitz. R., *Information problem solving: the big six approach to library and information skills instruction*, Ablex, 1990. Website:
http://edweb.sdsu.edu/edfirst/bigsix/basics.html

Hackett, S. and Kennedy, B., *Managing school IT*, Cambridge, Pearson, 1996.

Hanson, K., *Webwhacking? Issues for an Internet paradigm*. In press.

Harris, R., *Evaluating Internet research sources*. Website:
http://www.sccu.edu/faculty/R_Harris/evalu8it.htm

Heinrich, P., 'The school development plan for IT', in Tagg, B. (ed.), *Developing a whole school IT policy*, London, Pitman, 1995.

Heppel, S., 'Issues for a future curriculum', in School Curriculum and Assessment Authority, *Information technology, communications and the future curriculum: international conference report*, London, SCAA, 1997.

Herring, J. E. (ed.), *Information technology in schools*, London, Library Association Publishing, 1992.

Herring, J. E., *Teaching information skills in schools*, London, Library Association Publishing, 1996.

Herring, J. E., 'Press for action', *Educational computing and technology*, May 1998, 49–51.

Herring, J. E., 'School informatics: the vision, the learning, the information, the technology and the need for research', paper presented at the 2nd Annual Forum on Research in School Librarianship, 27th IASL Conference, Israel, 1998.

Intranet communicator, **1** (8), 1997, 31.

Johnson, D., 'Student access to the Internet', *Emergency librarian*, **22** (3), 1995, 8–12.

Johnson, D. and Eisenberg, M., 'Computer skills for information problem solving: learning and teaching technology in context', *ERIC digest*, **23** (5), March 1996.

Jones, R., 'The management of resources: IT in the library', *School libraries in view*, (6), Autumn 1996, 3–5.

Kenny, J., 'A fair share of the Web', *Times educational supplement online education*, 9 January 1998.

Kuhlthau, C., *Virtual school library*, Libraries Unlimited, 1997.

Mackenzie, J., The wired classroom, 1998.

http://www.fromnowon.org/mar98/flotilla.html

Marland, M. (ed.), *Information skills in the secondary curriculum*, London, Methuen, 1981.

McMurdo, G., 'HTML for the lazy', *Journal of information science*, **22** (3) 1996, 198–212.

Means, B., Plugging in, 1998.

http://www.nerel.org/sdrs/edtalk/toc.htm

Millard, E., *Developing readers in the middle years*, Milton Keynes, Open University Press, 1994.

Mitsubishi Electric (1997), *Intranet: the business benefits*, Birmingham, Mitsibushi Electric, 1997.

National Council for Educational Technology, *Information sheet on IT policy*, Coventry, NCET. 1996.

National Council for Educational Technology, *Libraries of the future: final report*, Coventry, NCET, 1996.

Nielson, J., Top ten mistakes in Web design, 1996.

http://www.useit.com/alertbox/9605.html

Pitts, H., 'The school office', in Tagg, B., *Developing a whole school IT policy*, London, Pitman, 1995.

Radford, T., 'No small potatoes', *Online guardian*, 23 July 1998, 9–10.

Raouf, F., 'Is this the end of the CD?', *Viglen magazine*, (13), Winter 1997/8, 8.

School Curriculum and Assessment Authority, *An introduction to the revised National Curriculum*, London, SCAA, 1995.

Schwier, R., *Interactive multimedia instruction*, New Jersey, Educational Technology Publications, 1993.

Scott, E., *Managing the Internet in the school library*, London, School Library Association, 1997.

Smith, M., 'The IT audit', in Tagg, B., *Developing a whole school IT policy*, London, Pitman,1995.

Tate, N., 'Introduction and welcome', in School Curriculum and Assessment Authority, *Information technology, communications and the future curriculum: international conference report*, London, SCAA, 1997.

Treadaway, M., 'Information capability 2000? A peek into the future', *School library 2000*, **10**, March 1996, 1, 20.

Wray, D. and Lewis, M., *Extending literacy*, London, Routledge, 1997.

Wray, D. and Lewis, M., *Practical ways to teach reading for information*, London, Routledge, 1997.

Index